SCOTT, FORESMAN ENGLISH

IN TUNE

BOOK 3

IN TUNE

BOOK 3

Manuel C. R. dos Santos

Centro Internacional de Línguas
Curitiba, Paraná, Brazil

Scott, Foresman and Company

Editorial Offices: Glenview, Illinois

Regional Offices: Palo Alto, California · Tucker, Georgia
Glenview, Illinois · Oakland, New Jersey · Dallas, Texas

Art by Tom Dunnington.
Cover illustration by Andrea Eberbach.

ISBN: 0-673-19103-6

11121314-DOC-01009998

I would like to acknowledge my good fortune in
having had such a wonderful team of editors
working with me on this project, and a wife like

HELOISA

whose constant encouragement, criticism, and
dedication to the program have been a very
special kind of "coauthorship."

Thank you, too, my sons, for putting up with me
during the three years of writing and composing,
and for giving up time which normally would
have been yours.

The Author

Contents

Using the Cue Book

Student
Book

You will use the Cue Books for
many exercises. Here's how:

Cue Book

---

1. Put the Cue Book
next to your
Student Book.

---

2. Look at the exercise
in the Student Book.

---

3. Open the Cue Book
to the Chart
mentioned in the
exercise directions.

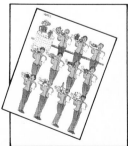

---

4. Read the directions in the Student Book. Look in the Cue Book to find the picture that has the number mentioned in the directions. (NOTE: We don't always begin with Picture 1.).

Ask and Answer. Use Cue Book Chart 2. Start with **1.** Answer *ad lib.*

   STUDENT A: I don't like tea. Do you?
   STUDENT B: Yes, I do. *or:* No, I don't.

5. Continue, matching the Cue Book pictures with the boldface numbers in the exercise.

Ask and answer. Use Cue Book Chart 2. Start with **1.** Answer *ad lib.*

   STUDENT A: I don't like tea. Do you?
   STUDENT B: Yes, I do. *or:* No, I don't.
   STUDENT C: I don't like coffee. Do you?
   STUDENT D: Yes, I do. *or:* No, I don't.
   STUDENT E: I don't like hamburgers. Do you?
   STUDENT F: . . . etc.

LESSON 1

CONVERSATION

	RICK:	Brent Wood!
	BRENT:	Rick Stevens! Good to see you!
	RICK:	Yes, it's been a long time, hasn't it?
	BRENT:	I don't think we've seen each other since college, have we?
5		And that was a long time ago! What's new?
	RICK:	Well, I have a wife and three kids, and we have our own
		business. I'm really very happy. How about you?
	BRENT:	Well, I'm still single. I guess the right woman hasn't
		found me yet. I'm a lawyer with Jenkins and Townsend.
10		I've been with them for nine years. We have business
		all over the country, so I have to travel a lot. I love the
		work because I meet so many kinds of people and I have to
		solve all kinds of problems. But you said you and your wife
		have your own business. Tell me about it.
15	RICK:	We make toys—old-fashioned toys. Nothing electric. You know,
		nowadays kids don't think; the toys think for them. Our factory
		is still small, but it's growing all the time.
	BRENT:	Well, I certainly wish you the best of luck. I'm sure you'll be a
		success.
20	RICK:	Thanks. By the way, have you seen any of our old[1] college friends?
	BRENT:	Yes, wherever I go I find somebody. About two weeks ago I met
		Bess Brown in L.A. She's become an actress, you know.
	RICK:	No!
	BRENT:	Yeah, and whenever I go to Boston I always stay with Robert. He's a
25		computer programmer. How about you? Do you see anybody?
	RICK:	Only Mike Thomas. He married a seventy-year-old woman.
	BRENT:	You're kidding!
	RICK:	I'm not, but she died a year later and left him . . .
	BRENT:	A fortune!
30	RICK:	No, a lot of bills.
	BRENT:	Poor[2] Mike! He never was very lucky, was he? Well, I have to go now.
		I have an appointment at 5:00. It was nice talking to you, Rick.
	RICK:	Likewise. Keep in touch!
	BRENT:	You too, and take care.

---

[1] Here, *old* = *from the past.* The friends may be young or old.
[2] Here, *poor* = *having a lot of problems or trouble.* Mike may be rich or poor.

(repairman) (computer programmer) (lawyer) (judge) (soldier) (sailor) (fisherman) (toys) (carpenter) (cashier) (farmer) (tour guide) (plumber) (firefighter) (electrician)

DEFINITIONS

all over: everywhere.

by the way: We say this when we remember something and want to change the conversation.

college: university. A university is larger than a college. NOTE: We usually use the word college: *Where did you go to college? When I was in college . . .*, etc.

fortune: a lot of money.

to grow / grew / grown: to become bigger (*My flowers are growing*); to put flowers or vegetables in the ground and then look after them while they grow (*I'm growing flowers*).

Keep in touch: Write or call on the phone.

kid: *(colloquial)* child.

likewise: I think or feel the same as you do.

luck: what you have if you are lucky.

to marry / married / married: to get married to.

old: not young (*an old professor*); not new (*an old college*); from the past (*my old professor; my old college*).

own: if something is yours and nobody else's it is *your own.* The word always comes after a possessive.

poor: not rich; having problems or trouble.

to solve / solved / solved: to find answers to problems.

whatever / whenever / wherever / whoever: See Grammar Summary.

You're kidding!: Really?!

MINI-CONVERSATION 1

A: Hello, Mike. Where have you been? I haven't seen you for years.
B: I've been in jail.
A: You're kidding! What happened?
B: First I robbed a bank, then I shot a police officer, and then . . .
A: Well, it was nice talking to you, Mike. Take care . . . and keep in touch.

MINI-CONVERSATION 2

A: Where should we go this evening?
B: Wherever you like, darling.
A: What should I wear?
B: Whatever you like.
A: Who should we invite to go with us?
B: Whoever you want to invite.
A: What time should we go?
B: Whenever you want to go.
A: Are you all right, Pete?

CONVERSATION PRACTICE

About the Conversation

1. When did Brent last see Rick?   2. How many children does Rick have?   3. Is Brent married?   4. What does he do?   5. Does he enjoy his job? Why?   6. What does Rick do?   7. What's his factory like?   8. Who does Brent stay with whenever he goes to Boston? What does Brent's friend do?   9. Who did Mike Thomas marry? Was she rich? Do you think he thought she was rich?   10. Why does Brent have to leave so soon?

Situation

You meet an old friend in the street. You haven't seen each other for years. Talk about your jobs, families, other old friends, etc.

SUMMARY OF NEW WORDS

VERBS: REGULAR

to marry / married / married   to solve / solved / solved

VERBS: IRREGULAR

to grow / grew / grown

NOUNS

carpenter(s)	fisherman (fishermen)	plumber(s)
cashier(s)	fortune(s)	repairman (repairmen)
college(s)	judge(s)	sailor(s)
computer programmer(s)	kid(s)	soldier(s)
electrician(s)	lawyer(s)	tour guide(s)
farmer(s)	luck	toy(s)
firefighter(s)		

ADJECTIVES

old   own   poor

ADVERBS

all over   whenever   wherever

PRONOUNS

whatever   whoever

EXERCISES

A. Ask and answer. Use Cue Book Chart 3. Answer *ad lib*. Start with *to earn / more / 7 / 8*.

STUDENT A: Who earns more, a judge or a firefighter?
STUDENT B: I think a judge earns more than a firefighter.

1. to work / harder / **9** / **10**
2. to travel / more / **11** / **12**
3. to drink / more / **13** / **14**
4. to speak / less / **1** / **2**
5. to earn / more / **3** / **4**
6. to work / less / **5** / TV **6**
7. to sit / more / **7** / **8**
8. to earn / more / **9** / **10**
9. to stand / more / **11** / **12**

B. Help them solve their problems. Use Cue Book Chart 3. Start with *I want to leave my husband / see / **1***.

STUDENT A: I want to leave my husband.
STUDENT B: You should see a lawyer.

1. The lamp is broken / take it to / **2**
2. My closet door doesn't open / look for / **3**
3. I can't solve this problem / talk to / **4**
4. The kitchen faucet isn't working / call / **5**
5. Our vacuum cleaner is broken / take it to / **6**
6. We want to get married / see / **7**
7. I want to help other people / become / **8**
8. I want to grow a lot of vegetables / talk to / **9**
9. I want to find a good place to fish / ask / **10**
10. I'd like to cash a traveler's check / take it to / **11**
11. I don't know where the museum is / ask / **12**
12. I love a good fight / become / **13**
13. I just love the sea / be / **14**

Grammar Summary

Pronouns: Whatever / Whoever; *Adverbs:* Whenever / Wherever

Whatever = Anything (that) / Everything (that)
Whoever = Anyone (who) / Everyone (who)
Whenever = Any time / Every time
Wherever = Anywhere / Everywhere

You must do **whatever** he says.
Whoever solves the problem will win.
I see them **whenever** they come.
Wherever he is, I hope he's happy.

When we use these words with commands, they make the command stronger:

Whatever they pay you, do a good job. = Whatever they pay you, the most important thing is: Do a good job!

> Whoever you marry, love her more than anyone else. = Whoever you marry, the most important thing is: Love her more than anyone else!

DEVELOPING YOUR SKILLS

Use *whatever, wherever, whenever,* or *whoever.*

1. Mr. Brandt is a very friendly person. He meets new people ____ he goes.
2. My chest hurts ____ I breathe.
3. Mr. Wilson is a very good carpenter. He sells ____ he makes immediately.
4. Raul goes ____ Consuelo goes, and does ____ she does.
5. ____ said that is a fool.
6. I take the kids to the movies ____ I can.
7. We don't have any trouble with our little boy. He eats ____ we give him.
8. ____ happens, don't marry that man!
9. ____ solved that problem was very, very smart.
10. "In London or Timbuktu, or ____ you are, this is Peter Edwards saying, 'Good night!' "

Talk About Yourself

1. Describe your job. Do you enjoy it?   2. What job would you / wouldn't you like to have? Why?   3. What do you think of modern toys? Compare them to old-fashioned toys. Which are better? Why?   4. Do you like to grow flowers or vegetables? What kinds?   5. Talk about an old friend you haven't seen for a long time. Where does he / she live? What does he / she do—or don't you even know? What did you use to do together? Would you like to see him / her again? Why?

Test Yourself

What do you say in the following situations? (1 point each)

1. You are seeing someone for the first time. *(Good to see you. / Pleased to meet you.)*
2. A friend is going to live in another country. *(I guess you're going all over. / Keep in touch!)*
3. A friend of yours is starting a new business. *(Cheers! / I wish you the best of luck!)*
4. Someone is saying good-by. *(You're kidding! / Take care!)*
5. You and a friend are talking and suddenly you remember something that you want to tell him / her. *(What's wrong? / By the way . . .)*
6. You are meeting a friend after five years. *(Good to see you again. / Congratulations!)*
7. A friend has been working very hard. *(What do you look like? / You look tired.)*
8. A friend says he / she is happy to see you again. *(Thanks for calling. / Likewise.)*
9. A friend is inviting you to dinner. *(That's very kind of you. / That's quite all right.)*
10. Someone says he / she feels awful. *(How nice! / What a shame!)*

Total Score _____

What to say . . .

How are things?

I can't complain.

Song WHEN YOU COME HOME TO ME

D   G
I get up at dawn
A   D
And work until nine
Bm
Some people are born
E   A
To have a hard time
         E
5   But when you come home to me, baby
                      A
We light up the fire and turn off the TV.

D   G
I don't like my job
A   D
I can't stand this town
Bm
The traffic, the noise,
      E   A
10   The crowds get me down
         E
But when you come home to me, baby
                     A
We light up the fire and turn off the TV.

            G   A
What do you do when the sun doesn't shine?
           F♯m   B
What do you do when the weather's fine?
          Em   A   D   D7
15   What do you do every time I go away?

        G   A
I sit at home and wait by the phone
      F♯m   B
If I watch the game it isn't the same
     Em   A
I think about the things we do
        D   G A G A
From day to day.

D   G
Whenever I'm mad   20
A   D
I cry for a while
Bm
Whenever I'm sad
E   A
I think of your smile
         E
But then you come home to me, baby
                    A
We light up the fire and turn off the TV.   25

        D   G
Wherever I go
        A   D
Whatever I do
       Bm
Whoever I meet
       E   A
Just reminds me of you
          E
So whenever I'm free, baby   30
                     A
I light up the fire and turn off the TV.

           D
Oh, yes, I feel so free
      G   A
When you're with me
          D
Oh, yeah, I feel so free
      G   A
When you're with me.   35

LESSON 2

CONVERSATION 1

ROGER: Hello, Dennis, . . . Sally! Come in! Welcome to our new house!

SALLY: Thank you. It's a beautiful place you have here.

ALICE: I'm glad you like it. Darling, will you serve drinks and show them the house while I finish dinner?

5 DENNIS: Do you need any help? You don't want to be alone in the kitchen, do you?

ALICE: Thanks, Dennis. That's quite all right.

● ● ●

ALICE: Please help yourselves if you'd like some more.

SALLY: It was delicious. You must give me the recipe.

10 ALICE: It was awfully easy. I just put it in the oven and it cooked itself.

DENNIS: Oh, come on, Alice! We all know you're an excellent cook.

● ● ●

DENNIS: I have another joke. Have you heard the one about the tramp who went into a department store and . . .

15 SALLY: Darling, it's getting terribly late. We really must go. Thanks for a lovely evening, Alice.

DENNIS: Yes, I don't think I've ever laughed so much.

SALLY: And at your own jokes too!

ALICE: We're so glad you could come.

20 ROGER: Yes, come again. *(Sally and Dennis leave.)* Oh! He's boring!

ALICE: Yes, I thought they'd never leave.

CONVERSATION 2

DENNIS: Can you give me something for indigestion?

PHARMACIST: Certainly, sir. Try Brand X tablets. You'll feel much better. And they're on sale. *(to another customer)* Now what can I do for you, miss?

5 CUSTOMER: I've had a sore throat for two days.

PHARMACIST: Take some Brand X and you'll be all right.

DENNIS: Why did you give us the same thing? I have indigestion and she has a sore throat.

PHARMACIST: Because it's the best product on the market. It'll cure

10 anything. I make it myself.

New Words

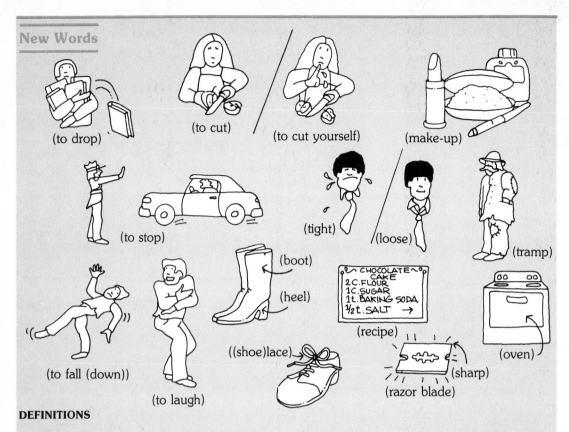

(to drop)

(to cut)

(to cut yourself)

(make-up)

(to stop)

(tight)

(loose)

(tramp)

(boot)

(heel)

(recipe)

CHOCOLATE CAKE
2 C. FLOUR
1 C. SUGAR
1 t. BAKING SODA
½ t. SALT →

(oven)

(to fall (down))

(to laugh)

((shoe)lace)

(sharp)

(razor blade)

DEFINITIONS

come on!: We use this expression when we want someone to tell what really happened.

to cure: to make someone well: *That medicine cured my cold/me.*

darn!: We use this expression when we are suddenly angry or have hurt ourselves.

excellent: very, very good.

to help yourself: to take food or a drink for yourself.

hit: a very popular show, movie, song, or record.

indigestion: stomachache because you ate too much or ate the wrong thing: *Fried food sometimes gives me indigestion.*

joke: short, funny story.

sale: when a store makes its prices lower for a few days, it is having *a sale*. Products with prices that are lower for a few days are *on sale*.

to serve: to give food and drinks to guests in your home or to customers in a restaurant.

sore: having pain.

to try: to work to do something; to taste something to find out if it's good or if it can help you.

to try on: to put something on to find out if you want to buy it.

welcome!: Be comfortable and happy in our home / country. We say this to guests when they arrive.

Who is it by? Who wrote it? or Who made the record? *The play was by Shakespeare. The song was by John Lennon. The record was by the Beatles.*

MINI-CONVERSATION 1

A: What was that?
B: It was me. I fell down the stairs.
A: Did you hurt yourself?
B: No, I'm OK.

MINI-CONVERSATION 2

A: I want to buy a record. Do you have "Stop Me If You Can"?
B: Who's it by?
A: By The Locomotion. It's their latest hit.
B: I'm afraid we don't.

MINI-CONVERSATION 3

A: Oh, darn! I've cut myself!
B: Now that wasn't very smart, was it? You know how sharp razors are. Here! I'll put something on it.
A: What?
B: Brand X, of course.

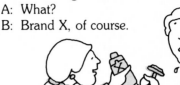

CONVERSATION PRACTICE

About Conversation 1

1. Have Dennis and Sally ever been to their friends' new house?   2. What does Sally think of the house?   3. What is Roger going to do while Alice finishes the dinner?   4. What kind of cook is Alice?   5. What does Sally want to get from Alice?   6. Why does she want to go?
7. Have you ever had a guest like Dennis? What did he / she do? Did he / she stay late?

About Conversation 2

1. What's the matter with Dennis?   2. What's wrong with the other customer?   3. How long has she had a sore throat?   4. What does the pharmacist give them?   5. Why does he say it's the best product on the market?

Situation 1

A friend of yours comes to visit you for the first time. You show him / her your house / apartment; ask him / her to stay for dinner, etc.

Situation 2

You work in a store. A customer comes in who wants to buy one of the following things: some new records, clothes, or furniture. He / She will describe what he / she wants. You don't have that, but perhaps he / she would like . . .

Situation 3

You are in a department store talking to a clerk. You want to see the manager to complain about something you bought. He / she arrives and wants to know when you bought it, what's wrong with it, if you still have the receipt, etc.

SUMMARY OF NEW WORDS

VERBS: REGULAR

to cure / cured / cured   to laugh / laughed / laughed   to stop / stopped / stopped

to drop / dropped / dropped   to serve / served / served   to try (on) / tried / tried

VERBS: IRREGULAR	ADJECTIVES			PRONOUNS
to cut / cut / cut	excellent	sharp	tight	See Grammar Summary
to fall (down) / fell / fallen	loose	sore		

NOUNS

boot(s)	hit(s)	joke(s)	oven(s)	recipe(s)	(shoe)lace(s)
heel(s)	indigestion	make-up	razor blade(s)	sale(s)	tramp(s)

PHRASES AND EXPRESSIONS

(Oh,) come on!   to help yourself   on sale   Who is it by?

Darn!   I thought they'd never leave   Welcome!

EXERCISES

A. What is each person saying? Use Cue Book Chart 1 and choose the correct sentence. Start with **15.**

1. **15** / Hold the line! / I can't hear you.
2. **16** / Did you hurt yourself? / I can't take you anywhere.
3. **17** / SALESWOMAN: What do you think you're doing? / Can I help you?
   CUSTOMER: Help yourself. / I'm just looking.
4. **18** / CUSTOMER: Can I take this purse home? / Do you have another color?
   SALESWOMAN: I'm afraid we don't. / Of course not!
5. **19** / CUSTOMER: How much are they? / Can I put these on?
   SALESMAN: No, they're mine. / 50 Q.
6. **20** / CUSTOMER: These recipes are wrong. / These boots are too tight.
   SALESWOMAN: I'll get another pair then. / Don't you like high heels?
7. **22** / CUSTOMER: I'm afraid it's too small for me. / I don't like low beds.
   SALESMAN: We can look at a bigger one if you'd like. / That's your problem.
8. **23** / FIRST WOMAN: I'd like you to meet my boyfriend. / Where are you going?
   SECOND WOMAN: Who is he? / Pleased to meet you.
9. **24** / CUSTOMER: I'm good-looking, aren't I? / Do you have a smaller size?
   SALESMAN: I think so. / You look awful.
10. **25** / FIRST MAN: I like your underpants! / Oh, I apologize!
    SECOND MAN: That's very kind of you. / That's quite all right.
11. **1** / STORE DETECTIVE: What are you doing? / Help yourself!
    THIEF: Too bad. / Nothing.
12. **2** / I want some ice cream. / I can't find my mom.
13. **3** / This lamp is just what I wanted. / Welcome!
14. **4** / Could you come back later? / I'm afraid I don't have any change.
15. **6** / MAN: I'm terribly sorry. / You fool!
    WOMAN: You too. / It was my fault.

16. **7** / Going up! / Oh, come on!
17. **8** / Excuse me. Where are the stairs? / Can you lend me some money?
18. **10** / WOMAN: I want to complain about this hole in my sweater. / Is this in fashion?
      SALESWOMAN: Why don't you fix it yourself? / I'll call the manager.
19. **11** / SALESMAN: Enjoy yourselves! / Don't play with the toys!
      CHILDREN: Why not? / Thank you, sir.

B. Use Cue Book Chart 1.

1. **16** / What has just happened to the woman?
2. **17** / What is the customer doing?
3. **19** / What does the man want to know?
4. **21** / What is the woman buying?
5. **22** / What does the man need?
6. **24** / Why doesn't the man want the jacket?
7. **25** / What was the man doing inside?
8. **1** / What was the thief doing?
9. **2** / Why is the little boy crying?
10. **3** / What has the man bought?
11. **5** / Why are there so many people here?
12. **6** / What has the woman just done?
13. **9** / Why is the woman standing in front of the mirror?
14. **10** / Why is the woman complaining?
15. **11** / Why can't the children play with the toys?

Grammar Summary

Reflexive / Emphatic Pronouns

In reflexive sentences, the subject and object of the verb are the same person or thing:

I		**myself.**	We		**ourselves.**
You		**yourself.**	You	hurt	**yourselves.**
He	hurt	**himself.**	They		**themselves.**
She		**herself.**			
It		**itself.**			

We also use these pronouns to emphasize that the subject did the action:

    I fixed the car **myself.** = I did it alone and nobody helped me.
    The president **himself** came to the reception. = He didn't send another person.

NOTE: Sometimes we emphasize that the subject did the action alone by adding *by* or *all by* before the emphatic pronoun: *I fixed the car (all) by myself; The president came to the reception (all) by himself* (= no one came with him).

DEVELOPING YOUR SKILLS

Use the correct reflexive / emphatic pronoun.

1. There was nobody there to help her, so Mrs. Olsen carried the box ____.
2. We haven't enjoyed ____ so much in years.
3. The pharmacist made something for his indigestion ____.
4. Don't wait for me; please help ____. I always want my guests to feel comfortable.
5. They were very lucky when they had the accident. They didn't hurt ____ at all.
6. We rarely eat out. I prefer to cook ____.
7. Tommy is crying because he cut ____.
8. I won't do it for you and you don't really need my help. Why don't you do it all by ____?
9. Have you heard about Mary? She killed ____.
10. That's a beautiful dress you're wearing. Did you make it ____?

Reading

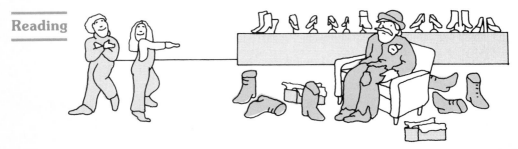

An old tramp walked into the shoe department of a large store and sat down. His clothes were old, his shoes didn't have any laces, and his socks were full of holes. He wore a hat that was too small for him and an enormous red flower on his jacket.

Soon a saleswoman came. "Can I help you, sir?" she asked. "I'd like a pair of boots, miss,"
5 the tramp answered. The woman asked about the size, color, and style he wanted and brought him some boots. The tramp tried on one pair after another. Some were too tight; others were too loose. Some were comfortable, but too big. Some had very high heels; others were too low. Some had laces; some didn't. But there was always something wrong with every pair he tried on.

While he was trying on the boots two children sat down opposite him. Whenever the old
10 tramp put on a new pair of boots, the children laughed. The tramp became angrier and angrier. "I've had enough," he shouted and ran after them—across the store, down the stairs, out the door, and into the street. When they turned the corner the children stopped. The tramp stopped too. "Thanks, kids! These are just great," he said. "Now I need another jacket and a new pair of pants. Maybe a nice warm pair of socks too. And then I'll be ready for winter."

About the Reading

1. Where did the tramp go? 2. What was he wearing? 3. Was he a young man? 4. What did he want to get? 5. What did the saleswoman want to know before she brought him the boots? 6. Did he try on many pairs of boots? Why? 7. Where did the children sit? 8. Why did the tramp become angry? 9. What did he do? 10. Why did the tramp thank the children? 11. What did he still need? 12. What was he getting ready for? 13. Do you think he'll come back to the same store for the other clothes? Why?

Writing

Write the conversation between the saleswoman and the tramp.

Talk About Yourself

1. Do you like to invite friends for dinner?   2. Can you cook? What's your favorite recipe? Can you describe how you make it?   3. Do you have tramps in your city? Are they a problem? What do they do?   4. Do you like to go to department stores? Why?   5. Why do people sometimes steal things from department stores?   6. Have you ever seen anyone who was stealing from a store? What happened? Did you do anything?

Test Yourself

Use the correct reflexive / emphatic pronouns and choose the right word in the following sentences. (1/2 point each)

1. A: What's so *(sharp / funny)?*
   B: Have you looked at ____ in the mirror?
2. The *(whole / hole)* country will know I did it all by ____.
3. These mushrooms *(taste / feel)* fine! Did you cook them ____?
4. We only stayed there *(for / during)* two days, but we really enjoyed ____.
5. The hotel ____ is beautiful, but the *(service / work)* is awful.
6. Sometimes when my aunt was very *(worried / sore)* she used to talk to ____.
7. After the accident my hand was *(loose / sore).* I couldn't even dial a phone ____.
8. The children washed their socks all by ____ and then *(tried them on / put them on).*
9. Doctor Barnes gave the pharmacist the *(recipe / prescription)* ____.
10. The bank manager ____ *(borrowed / lent)* me the money.

Total Score _____

What to say . . .

Enjoying yourself, dear?

LESSON 3

CONVERSATION 1   *Mr. Juarez's office in Mexico City.*

RAMIREZ: Sorry to trouble you, sir.
JUAREZ: That's quite all right. Sit down. Have you arranged every-
thing for tomorrow?
RAMIREZ: I think so, sir. I've hired interpreters. Don't worry.
5 JUAREZ: What do you mean, don't worry? Remember, Ramirez, these
Russian politicians are VIP's,[1] so I don't want any mistakes.

CONVERSATION 2   *In the plane.*

PILOT: Good morning, ladies and gentlemen. This is your captain.
We'd like to welcome you aboard Utopia Airlines Flight 709 to
Mexico City. We are flying at an altitude of 20,000 feet, and
our speed is 700 miles an hour. Our flight will take approxi-
5 mately three hours, and we expect to arrive at 2 P.M. Mexico
City time. The temperature in Mexico City is 20°C.
BUDDY: Hi, neighbor. I'm Buddy Hick. And this is my wife, Mary Beth.
RON: Hello, Buddy. Hello, Mary Beth. I'm Ron Sandstead.
MARY BETH: Howdy, Ron!
10 BUDDY: We're on a tour. I've always wanted to go to Mexico. Man!
I'm really looking forward to this vacation.
MARY BETH: So am I. I read about Machu Picchu when I was at school.
RON: But Machu Picchu is in Peru.
MARY BETH: Oh! Well, maybe we're going there too.

CONVERSATION 3   *At the airport.*

BUDDY: Look, Mary Beth. "WELCOME TO MEXICO." Isn't that nice?
MARY BETH: It sure is. Now smile, dear! We're going to have our pictures[2] in
the papers.[3] I can't wait to tell the folks back home about this.
ATTENDANT: Excuse me, ma'am. Would you please get out of the way?
5 The reporters are trying to take some photos of these Russian
gentlemen.

---

[1] VIP's = very important people.
[2] Here, *pictures = photographs.*
[3] Here, *papers = newspapers.*

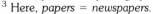

New Words

(to smile)

(in the way)

(out of the way)

(degrees)

(near)

(far (from))

(camper)

(to drown)

(to sail)

(tent)

(to surf)

(litter)

(sand)

(fire)

(campground)

DEFINITIONS

altitude: how high something is over the sea: *Mexico City is at an altitude of approximately 7,400 feet.*

approximately: about.

to arrange (for / to): to make all of the plans for something: *She arranged for the party; He arranged to buy all the food.*

back home: We use this expression to speak about our hometown when we are not there.

to be called: the name of a person, place, or thing is what it is called.

to camp: to sleep outdoors or in a tent; to go to a campground.

can't wait: We use this expression when we are happy because we want to do something soon or want something to happen soon: *I can't wait to go camping; They can't wait for the party.*

captain: pilot.

change: when you change something, you make a change.

crowded: full of people or things: *The reception was awfully crowded; My dresser looks crowded, doesn't it?*

dear: darling.

folks: *(colloquial)* people you know or family.

to go camping / sailing: to go to a place where you can camp / sail.

to hire: to give someone a job; to pay to use something: *I hired a new saleswoman; They should hire a taxi.*

howdy: *(colloquial)* How do you do?

industry: all of one kind of business: the airline industry, the real estate industry, the tourist industry, etc.

to look forward to: to be excited about something that is going to happen.

to mean: to intend to say: *When I said it was raining, I meant you should bring your umbrella; The word "rich" means "not poor."*

neither: not one and not the other.

souvenir: something you buy on a trip for yourself or for someone else. It helps you remember the trip or tells the other person you thought of him / her while you were traveling.

speed: how fast something goes or is going.

to spend (on): to use money or time: *I spent all my money on souvenirs; How did you spend your time when you were in Mexico?*

tour: a trip to many places (often with many other people). A travel agency arranges tours.

tourism: the tourist industry.

to trouble: to ask a question that makes trouble or work for somebody else.

village: a very small town.

to welcome: to say "welcome" or "hello" when someone arrives; to be happy to see someone.

Welcome aboard!: we say this to welcome someone on a plane, boat, etc.

MINI-CONVERSATION 1

A: Hello. Smith's Travel Agency.
B: Hello, Peggy. Don Reed here. There's been a change in our plans. We'd like to take the evening flight. Can you arrange it?
A: I'll see what I can do. . . . Yes, you're OK.
B: Thanks a lot, Peggy. Sorry to trouble you.
A: No problem. Good-by.

MINI-CONVERSATION 2

A: Excuse me. How far is the campground?
B: About two miles down this road. But it's very crowded there. You can camp in our yard if you'd like.
A: Oh, that's very kind of you.
B: That'll be 20 Q for the tent, 5 Q for a shower, 2 Q for the soap . . .
A: I thought you were a friendly farmer. I didn't know you worked for the camping industry.

CONVERSATION PRACTICE

About Conversation 1

1. What does Ramirez say when he comes in? 2. What does Juarez say? 3. Who is arriving? 4. Is Ramirez sure that everything will be OK?

About Conversations 2–3

1. Why are Buddy and Mary Beth going to Mexico? Do they know if they're going to Peru? 2. Are they looking forward to their vacation? 3. Why is Mary Beth excited when they arrive at the airport? 4. Why are the reporters at the airport?

Situation 1

You and a friend are planning a trip. Talk about your plans and describe where you want to go, what you will do, where you will stay, what you will need, etc.

You want to change your flight: day, time, airline, etc. Call your travel agent and arrange for the change.

SUMMARY OF NEW WORDS

VERBS: REGULAR

to arrange (for / to) / arranged / arranged
to camp / camped / camped
to drown / drowned / drowned

to hire / hired / hired
to sail / sailed / sailed
to smile / smiled / smiled

to surf / surfed / surfed
to trouble / troubled / troubled
to welcome / welcomed / welcomed

VERBS: IRREGULAR		PRONOUNS	ADJECTIVES
to mean / meant / meant	to spend (on) / spent / spent	neither	crowded

NOUNS

			ADVERBS
altitude	fire(s)	souvenir(s)	approximately
camper(s)	folks	speed	far (from)
campground(s)	industry (industries)	tent(s)	in the way
captain(s)	litter	tour(s)	out of the way
change(s)	Peru	tourism	
degree(s)	sand	village(s)	

PHRASES AND EXPRESSIONS

back home	dear	in / out of the way
to be called	to go camping / sailing	to look forward to
can't wait (to / for)	howdy	Welcome aboard!

EXERCISES

Use Cue Book Chart 2. Answer *ad lib.*

Why is the beach crowded? *Because it's the weekend / summer* or *because the weather's fine* or . . .

1. **1** / What kind of music do you think they're listening to?
2. **2** / Who do you think was sitting here? What did they do? What kind of people were they?
3. **3** / Why is the smaller boy crying? Do you think the fat boy should eat ice cream? Why?
4. **4** / Why has the bus stopped?
5. **5** / Who has just arrived at the hotel?
6. **6** / Why is the restaurant empty?
7. **7** / Is the bus service good? How do you know?
8. **8** / Why is the old woman running?
9. **9** / Why do you think they're leaving?
10. **10** / Did Mrs. Baker come to the beach alone? How do you know?
11. **11** / Whose children are they? What are they doing?

12. **12** / What does the man in the water need? Why?
13. **13** / Why is Mrs. Collins sitting alone?
14. **14** / Why are so many people buying the newspaper?
15. **15** / Why are the man and woman arguing?
16. **16** / What kinds of things do they sell in this store?
17. **17** / Where are the boys playing?
18. **18** / Why is Mr. Bass so sad?
19. **19** / Have you ever gone sailing? Where? When? Did you enjoy it?
20. **20** / Can they surf well? Can you surf? Have you ever tried? Did you enjoy it?
21. **21** / Who do you think is going to win? Why?
22. **22** / Describe the campground. Why do you think it's so crowded?

Grammar Summary

Pronoun + Of

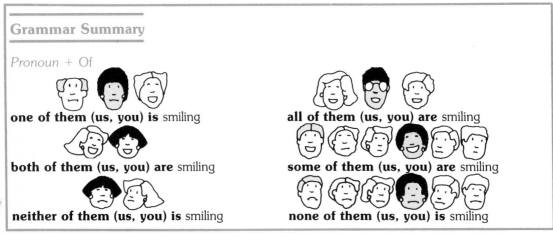

one of them (us, you) is smiling

both of them (us, you) are smiling

neither of them (us, you) is smiling

all of them (us, you) are smiling

some of them (us, you) are smiling

none of them (us, you) is smiling

DEVELOPING YOUR SKILLS

Use *one, both, neither, some, all,* or *none* in the following questions about Cue Book Chart 2.

1. **1** / ____ of them are young.
2. **3** / ____ of them is crying.
3. **4** / ____ of them are taking photos.
4. **7** / ____ of them are waiting.
5. **11** / ____ of them is swimming.

6. **12** / ____ of them is in trouble.
7. **13** / ____ of them wears glasses.
8. **14** / ____ of them want newspapers.
9. **15** / ____ of them will say "It was my fault."
10. **17** / ____ of them is sitting down.

Reading

Some of them come by bus or train;
Some by car; others by plane;
Some come on boats and some by bike,
And there are even those who hike.*
Some bring their cats and dogs and birds—
Foreigners, all using different words—
Some speaking languages you've never heard.

5

*To hike = to go for a long walk.

Tourism began in the nineteenth century. A young man called Thomas Cook hired a train to take some people to a meeting in a town nearby. Trains were new then, and everybody thought the trip was very exciting. Soon Cook started the first travel agency. He arranged "package tours,"* and his business grew very quickly. Since that time, tourism has become one of the world's largest industries. Nowadays there are towns—and even countries—that live because of tourism. This means that most of their money comes from tourists who visit there.

Stores, restaurants, and hotels welcome tourists, because people on vacation normally spend their money more easily. But the people who live in towns that have a lot of tourists don't usually like them. They mean noise, litter, a higher cost of living, and very often a change in the lives of the people and in the towns themselves. Zeke McDonald of Highland Springs, a popular tourist area, says: "I'm tired of all these tourists. That's why I spend my vacation far from home in a beautiful little village near the sea. We drive along a sand road and it takes us a day to get there. I tell everybody it's a terrible place, so people think I'm crazy. I just hope none of those travel agents ever finds it."

About the Reading

1. Who is the writer talking about in the first seven lines?   2. Why did Cook need a train?
3. Did the people enjoy themselves? Why?   4. What did Cook start?   5. Why do you think his business grew so quickly?   6. Is tourism important nowadays? Why?   7. Why do the hotel and restaurant industries like tourists?   8. Do the people who live in popular tourist areas like the people who visit there? Why?   9. Where does Zeke McDonald spend his vacation? Why?
10. Why does he tell everyone it's a terrible place?   11. Do you have many tourists in your town / country? What do most of them visit when they come?   12. Do the people in your town / country like them? Why?

Writing

Write about a vacation or tour you went on.

Talk About Yourself

1. Which of these vacations would / wouldn't you like to have? Why / Why not?   2. What are the good or bad things about them?

*Package tour = a tour that a travel agent arranges and you pay for before you leave.

Which one means the same thing? (1 point each)

1. What's new?
   What new things have you bought? / Has anything interesting happened lately?
2. Please get out of the way.
   Please leave the house! / I can't see. You're standing in front of me.
3. I have my hands full.
   I have a lot of things in my hands. / I'm very busy.
4. Welcome aboard!
   I'm the captain. / We're glad to have you with us.
5. Help yourself.
   You need help. / Take something if you'd like it.
6. I'm looking forward to that.
   I'm looking in front of me. / I'm excited about something.
7. Sorry to trouble you.
   I'm sorry you're in trouble. / Do you mind if I ask a question?
8. Ouch!
   Someone just kissed me. / I hurt myself.
9. What does he look like?
   What does he like to look at? / Is he good-looking?
10. Can I take your order?
    What do you want to do? / What would you like to eat?

Total Score _____

What to say . . .

SORRY TO TROUBLE YOU, BUT MAY I USE YOUR PHONE?

LESSON 4

CONVERSATION 1

MECHANIC: Good morning. What can we do for you, ma'am?

MAUREEN: I'm afraid there's something wrong with my car. It won't go very fast and it makes a strange noise.

MECHANIC: Is it using a lot of gas?

5   MAUREEN: Oh, yes. I filled the tank two days ago and it's already empty. And I haven't really driven very much.

MECHANIC: We'll have a look at it for you. You probably have some dirt in the carburetor.

MAUREEN: Will you be able to fix it this afternoon?

10 MECHANIC: It depends. If it's only the carburetor, you can pick it up in an hour.

MAUREEN: I'll come back later then.

● ● ●

MAUREEN: Is my car ready?

MECHANIC: I'm afraid not. We cleaned your carburetor, but we'll have to change the battery, fix a hole in the radiator, open the engine . . . It's serious. We won't be able to have it ready before tomorrow evening. I'm afraid it's going to cost you a fortune. I suggest you get a new car.

15

CONVERSATION 2

PETE: Good afternoon, sir.

ZEKE: Hello. I want to rent a car for a day or two. Do you have a medium-sized one available?

PETE: Yes. It'll cost you 450 Q a day plus 1 Q a kilometer.

5   ZEKE: I plan to visit my folks in Boswell. Will I be able to leave the car there?

PETE: No, I'm afraid you'll have to return it to us here.

ZEKE: Will I have to pay a deposit?

PETE: Yes, 25 Q.

10 ZEKE: Do you need anything else?

PETE: I'll need to see your driver's license.

ZEKE: I don't have one, but I can drive very well.

PETE: Sorry, sir, but no driver's license, no car!

New Words

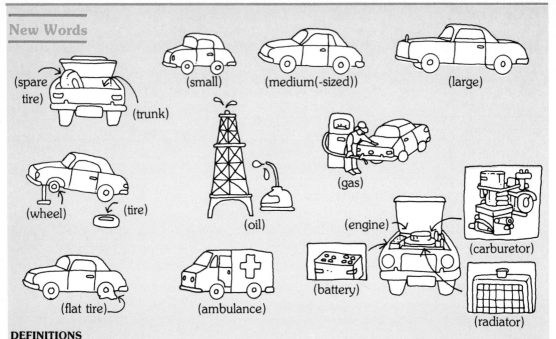

(spare tire) (trunk) (small) (medium(-sized)) (large)

(wheel) (tire) (oil) (gas) (engine) (carburetor)

(flat tire) (ambulance) (battery) (radiator)

DEFINITIONS

available: you can get it.

back: to a place where something or someone was before or to the person who had it. See Grammar Summary.

to be able: can.

to break down: when something breaks down it won't work anymore.

to check: to see if something is all right.

damn!: We use this expression when we are very angry. Many people don't use or like to hear this word; they think it's not nice.

deposit: when you put money in the bank, you *make a deposit;* when you rent something, you *pay a deposit* to be sure that you will return the thing that you have rented. (When you bring the thing back, they give your deposit back to you.)

dirt: what makes things dirty; what flowers grow in.

to fill: to make something full.

fill it up: fill the tank with gas.

in an hour (minute, week, month, etc.): after an hour (minute, week, month, etc.).

including: with; you don't have to pay more to have the thing.

in fact: actually.

insurance: if you have car insurance, the insurance company pays if you have an accident; if you have life insurance, they pay your family if you die.

it depends: I'm not sure; maybe.

to keep warm (hot, cold): to help something or someone stay at the right temperature: *I put the meat in the oven to keep it hot; You'll have to wear a jacket to keep warm.*

noise: what makes something noisy.

plenty (of): enough.

plus: not including; also.

probably: not just maybe, but not certainly either.

to return: to bring something back; to come back.

to run out of: not to have any more of; to use all of.

service station: where you go to get gas and oil for your car, to put air in the tires, etc.

to suggest: to make a suggestion.

tank: where the gas is in a car.

warranty: when you buy a car, washing machine, etc., you get a six-month or a year's warranty. This means that the company promises to fix it if it breaks down or if there is a problem during the first six months or the first year.

MINI-CONVERSATION 1

A: Yes, sir?

B: Fill it up, please. And could you check the water, the battery, the oil, and the tires?

A: Yes, sir.

MINI-CONVERSATION 2

A: There's nothing I can do, Juliet. It just broke down.

B: We've probably run out of gas.

A: There's plenty of gas. Can't you see? It just isn't working.

B: Oh, Romeo, are we going to have to spend the night here? I'm so cold!

A: Yes, I'm afraid we will. But don't worry. There are plenty of blankets in the trunk. And besides, I'll keep you warm.

MINI-CONVERSATION 3

A: Oh, damn!

B: What's wrong, darling?

A: I think we have a flat tire.

B: We can change it quickly and we'll still be able to get to the game.

A: I'm afraid you're wrong. We don't have a spare.

MINI-CONVERSATION 4

A: Hello. Mack's Service Station and Garage.

B: This is Roy Slater speaking. Is my car ready yet?

A: I'm afraid we haven't been able to find out what's wrong with it. I think you need a new car, Mr. Slater.

B: Or maybe a new garage!

CONVERSATION PRACTICE

About Conversation 1

1. What does Maureen say is wrong with her car?   2. How long ago did she fill the tank?
3. What does the mechanic think is wrong?   4. Will he be able to fix it immediately?   5. What will they have to do to Maureen's car?   6. Will they be able to do it before tomorrow night?
7. What does the mechanic suggest?   8. How long has she had the car?   9. Do you think there are really so many things wrong with the car?   10. What do you think Maureen is going to do?

About Conversation 2

1. How big a car does Zeke want to rent?   2. How much will it cost?   3. Why does Zeke want

to leave the car in Boswell?   4. Will he be able to do this?   5. What will he have to do instead?
6. What else will Zeke have to pay?   7. What must he show Pete before he can take the car?
8. Why do you think Zeke doesn't have a driver's license?

Situation 1

You are at a garage. Tell the mechanic what's wrong with your car. He / She tells you what
he / she thinks is wrong and what he / she will have to do. Ask how much it will cost and when
the car will be ready.

Situation 2

You took your car to a garage. Two days after they fixed it you have the same problem. Speak
to the manager and complain about the service.

SUMMARY OF NEW WORDS

VERBS: REGULAR		POLITE FORMS
to check / checked / checked	to return / returned / returned	could
to fill / filled / filled	to suggest / suggested / suggested	

VERBS: IRREGULAR

	ADVERBS	PREPOSITIONS
to be able / was (were) able / been able	back	including
to break down / broke down / broken down	probably	plus

NOUNS

ambulance(s)	engine(s)	oil	tire(s)
battery (batteries)	gas	radiator(s)	trunk(s)
carburetor(s)	insurance	service station(s)	warranty (warranties)
deposit(s)	kilometer(s)	spare(s)	wheel(s)
dirt	noise(s)	tank(s)	

ADJECTIVES

available   flat   medium(-sized)   plenty (of)   spare

PHRASES

damn!	in + *time*	it depends	to run out of
fill it up	in fact	to keep (something) + *adj.*	

EXERCISES

A. Ask and answer. Use Cue Book Chart 4. Start with **4** / *What's Joe doing?*

> STUDENT A: What's Joe doing?
> STUDENT B: He's checking the tires.

1. **5** / What does the farmer have in his truck?
2. **6** / What will Mr. Harris have to do? Why?

3. **7** / Why wasn't Mrs. Lang able to get to the beach?
4. **8** / Has the mechanic been able to fix the car yet?
5. **9** / Was Bill able to have the car ready in time for Mr. Rich's meeting?
6. **10** / What does Mike have to do?
7. **1** / What did Mrs. Nelson have to do?
8. **2** / What does the police officer have to do with the thief?
9. **3** / What do you think the police officer wants Mr. Dean to do?

B. What are they saying to each other? Use Cue Book Chart 4.

1. **1 / 2** MRS. NELSON: Do you need any help? / How much, officer?
   OFFICER: Fill it up, please. / How much does gas cost?
2. **3 /** OFFICER: Please check the water and the oil. / The spare tire looks flat.
   MR. DEAN: Do you have a warranty? / Certainly, officer.
3. **4 / 5** BILL: What beautiful vegetables! / The engine looks dirty.
   FARMER: Oh, damn! I won't be able to get to the market. / This is nothing! You should see what we have on the farm.
4. **6 /** MR. HARRIS: I'm afraid I had a little accident. / When will you be able to fix my car?
   MS. BAKER: It depends. Maybe in a week. / You have insurance, of course, but we won't be able to give back your deposit.
5. **7 /** NANCY: Will we have to go back home? / Do you have insurance?
   MRS. LANG: I guess not. / Probably.
6. **8 /** MECHANIC: You just ran out of gas. / There's something wrong with the engine.
   MRS. LANG: Will you be able to fix it before 5 o'clock? / Why don't you fill the tank then?
7. **9 /** MR. RICH: Don't you have another car available? / How long will I have to wait?
   BILL: There's plenty of time. / Just a few minutes more.
8. **10 /** NURSE: Don't you have a spare tire? / I'll have to get to the hospital soon.
   MIKE: I'll do it as fast as I can. / Yes, there's one in the trunk.

Grammar Summary

1. Forms of Can / To Be Able

Can has only two forms: *can('t)* / *could(n't)*. *Can* is simple present; *could* is simple past. We usually use them with another verb:

   I **can** buy life insurance.
   I **could** buy life insurance when I was younger.

NOTE: We also use *can* to mean the future: *I can return the car tomorrow.* And we use *could* as a polite form of *can* to ask permission. It means the same thing as *may:*

Can			**can**		**can't**
Could	} I cash a check?	Yes, you {	**could.**	No, you {	**couldn't.**
May			**may.**		**may not.**

We use *to be able* with another verb in the infinitive form (the *to* form). We can use *to be able* in any tense or form:

I'm (not)
I was(n't)
I (didn't) use(d) to be
I've (I haven't) been
I'll (I won't) be
I'm (not) going to be
I'd (I wouldn't) be
} **able to cash** a check there.

2. *When to Use* Can/Could *and* To Be Able

We use *can/could* and *to be able* to mean ability or possibility:

ABILITY

He { **can**
is able to } swim.

He { **couldn't**
wasn't able to } swim.

POSSIBILITY

He { **can** (probably)
will (probably) **be able to** } fix the engine.

He (probably) { **couldn't**
wasn't able to } fix the engine.

For permission we use *can* or the polite forms *could/may*. We never use *to be able* for permission.

3. *Forms of* Must/Have to

The word *must* has only one form. We use it only to mean present or future:

I **must** change the tire { now.
later.

Like *to be able*, we can use *to have to* in all tenses and forms.

NOTE: In the negative, *mustn't* and *don't have to* mean different things:

You **mustn't** change the tire. = You **may not** change the tire!
You **don't have to** change the tire. = You **don't need to** change the tire.

4. The Adverb Back

We can use the adverb *back* with many verbs. Here are a few of them:
He gave me an umbrella, but he **wants** / **needs** it **back.** = He wants me to **give** the
    umbrella **back** to him.
The ambulance is **going** / **coming back** to the hospital.
I bought a blouse, but it's the wrong size. So I have to **take** / **bring** it **back.**
Now I must **walk** / **run** / **drive back** to the service station.

DEVELOPING YOUR SKILLS

A. Choose the correct form of the verb.

    Albert Reed is a millionaire's son. He *(never had / has never had)* to worry about any-
thing in his life. He *(was able / has been able)* to buy whatever he wants whenever he
wants. He *(doesn't have to / musn't)* work and he spends most of his time at the swimming
pool or riding in his brand new car. But he *(doesn't have to / mustn't)* drive himself; he has a
driver. Albert *(was never able / has never been able)* to get his driver's license. But next week
his life is going to change. He wants to show everybody that he *(can / could)* do something by
himself. He's going to become a soldier. After that, he *(has to / must)* get up early, eat all
kinds of food that he hates, wash his own clothes, and do many other things that he *(never
had / has never had)* to do. But perhaps that's just what he needs.

B. Use the picture to write six sentences using *will* / *won't be able to* and six sentences using
will / *won't have to.*

Writing

Write a letter to Drive-a-Car, 35 Hardy Road, Montreal, Quebec, Canada. Tell them:

1. You rented a car from them (give place and date, how long you had it).
2. You left the car at their office in Vancouver, where you told them you were going to leave it.
3. You paid everything, including . . .
4. Now you have gotten a bill and you are sure they have made a mistake.
5. You have the receipts.
6. Ask them to check their books.*

Talk About Yourself

1. Have you ever run out of gas? had a flat tire? rented a car? had trouble with a garage or service station? Tell about it.   2. When did you last take your car to a garage? What was wrong with it?   3. Is gas expensive in your country? Why or why not?   4. Have you ever driven without a license? Do many people drive without one in your country? What happens to them if the police find out?   5. How old must you be to get a driver's license? Is it hard to get one? What do you have to do to get one?

Test Yourself

Use the correct tense. (1 point each)

1. When Sandra finishes college she *(to be able)* to find a job easily.
2. I had no spare tire, so I *(to have to)* leave the car where it was.
3. He didn't die because the ambulance *(to be able)* to come immediately.
4. I'm afraid you *(must)* come back tomorrow, ma'am.
5. Mr. King couldn't work in Moronia because he *(−to be able)* to learn the language.
6. Our friends have paid for everything so we *(−to have to)* spend a Q since we arrived.
7. We always wanted to visit them, but unfortunately we *(−to be able)* to travel.
8. I *(−to have to)* work very hard but I do now.
9. Mary was never there so Pete *(can)* do whatever he wanted.
10. Unfortunately Mrs. Tanaka *(must)* leave next month.

Total Score _____

*A company's books tell everything important about their business during the last few years.

LESSON 5

CONVERSATION 1

MR. SCHMIDT:	I'd like to see Mr. Turner. My name is Klaus Schmidt from the International Research and Development Institute.
RECEPTIONIST:	Is Mr. Turner expecting you?
5 MR. SCHMIDT:	No, I'm afraid not.
RECEPTIONIST:	Have a seat. I'll see if Mr. Turner can see you now. *(on the phone)* Mr. Schmidt from IRDI would like to talk to you.
MR. TURNER:	I can't see him now. Ask him to come back later.
10 RECEPTIONIST:	I'm afraid Mr. Turner can't see you now. Can you come back later?
MR. SCHMIDT:	No, I can't. I'm busy all day.
RECEPTIONIST:	Would you like to see someone else instead?
MR. SCHMIDT:	No, I must talk to Mr. Turner himself. Can
15	you arrange an appointment for tomorrow?
RECEPTIONIST:	Let me see . . . yes . . . will ten o'clock be convenient?
MR. SCHMIDT:	Yes, ten o'clock will be fine. Thank you.

CONVERSATION 2

SECRETARY:	*(on the phone)* Mr. Powell's office.
MR. CHAMBERS:	Is Mr. Powell in?
SECRETARY:	No, he's out now. Would you like to leave a message?
MR. CHAMBERS:	Yes. Please tell him Mr. Chambers called and ask
5	him to meet me at four o'clock tomorrow afternoon. Oh, yes . . . ask him not to forget to bring the contracts. And tell him to be on time.
SECRETARY:	All right. Now . . . Mr. Chambers? Mr. Chambers! . . . Oh, no! He hung up.

● ● ●

10 MR. POWELL:	*(on the phone)* Hello, Mary. Any messages?
SECRETARY:	Yes. Mr. Chambers called. He asked you to meet him at four o'clock tomorrow afternoon and to take the contracts. He also asked you not to be late.
MR. POWELL:	Where should I meet him?
15 SECRETARY:	I don't know. You see . . .
MR. POWELL:	You don't know! Why didn't you ask him?
SECRETARY:	I tried, but he didn't give me a chance.

New Words

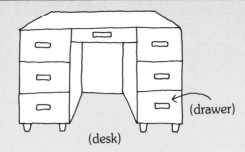

(drawer)

(desk)

DEFINITIONS

to be in / out: to be at home or in the office / not to be at home or in the office.

contract: a paper that two or more people sign that says both or all of them will do something.

convenient: at a time when you aren't planning to do something else.

to discuss: to talk about.

either . . . or: one thing or the other, but not both.

experience: what you know about something because you have done it for a long time.

fair: a special place where companies in one industry show their products for a few days.

to give someone a chance: to say someone may do something.

to have a seat: to sit down.

let me (him, her, etc.) know: tell me (him, her, etc.).

let me see: please wait while I check that or think about that.

marketing: in a business, the department that studies the sales of the company's products. It often makes suggestions about products, prices, showing products at fairs, etc.

matter: something important to discuss. *But remember:* What's the matter? = What's the problem?

message: what you tell someone to tell someone else.

on time: not early and not late, but just when it should happen.

order: what you tell a company you will buy from them.

pleased: happy about something.

report: what you say or write about something that happened or that you have seen, read, or done.

See you later: good-by.

urgent: when someone must do something immediately.

MINI-CONVERSATION 1

A: My name is Maureen Spencer. I have an appointment with Mr. Rosselli.

B: I'm afraid he's busy right now. He's at a meeting.

A: But I arranged to see him at four o'clock. How long will he be?

B: Probably about forty-five minutes.

A: That's too long. I have a meeting at five. Please ask him to call me either this evening or early tomorrow morning.

B: Does he have your number?

A: Yes, he does.

MINI-CONVERSATION 2

A: Martha, please type these orders and ask Jerry to bring me last month's reports. I have to go out now, so tell him to leave them on my desk.

B: Jerry, Mrs. Rich wants you to bring her last month's reports and to leave them on her desk.

C: Why doesn't she get them herself?

A: Because I asked *you* to get them, Jerry. See you later, Martha.

MINI-CONVERSATION 3

A: Mrs. Taylor, Mr. Parker's on the phone.

B: I have someone with me now. Tell him I'll call him later.

A: Mrs. Taylor is with someone now. Can she call you later?

C: I have a very urgent matter to discuss with her. Ask her to call me as soon as she's finished.

CONVERSATION PRACTICE

About Conversation 1

1. Who does Mr. Schmidt want to see? 2. Is Mr. Turner expecting him? 3. What does Mr. Turner ask Mr. Schmidt to do? 4. Can Mr. Schmidt come back later? Why not? 5. What does he want the receptionist to do? 6. What time is convenient for Mr. Schmidt?

About Conversation 2

1. Is Mr. Powell in his office? 2. What did Mr. Chambers ask Mr. Powell to do? 3. What did he ask Mr. Powell not to forget? 4. Where must Mr. Powell meet Mr. Chambers? 5. Why didn't Mr. Powell's secretary ask him?

Situation 1

You have a business appointment at 3 P.M. Unfortunately, your plane can't take off because of bad weather. You call the person, but he / she isn't in. You speak to his / her secretary and tell him / her why you won't be able to get there on time and when you expect to arrive. Ask him / her to call and tell your hotel you'll be late. Ask if someone can pick you up at the airport.

Situation 2

You have to speak to someone about an urgent matter. When you call, the person isn't there. Tell whoever answers why you are calling. Ask him / her to give the message to the other person.

SUMMARY OF NEW WORDS

VERBS: REGULAR	ADJECTIVES		
to discuss / discussed / discussed	convenient	pleased	urgent

NOUNS				CONJUNCTIONS
chance(s)	drawer(s)	marketing	order(s)	either . . . or
contract(s)	experience	matter(s)	report(s)	
desk(s)	fair(s)	message(s)		

to be in / out   to have a seat   to let someone know   See you later.
to give someone a chance   Let me see.   on time

EXERCISES

A. First tell what the person said, then make a command. Use *told* or *asked.* (Use *asked* when you think the person should or must be polite.) Start with *detective / thief / to drop his gun* or: *thief / detective / (−) to put him in jail.*

> STUDENT A: The detective told the thief to drop his gun.
> STUDENT B: Drop your gun!
> *or:* STUDENT A: The thief asked the detective not to put him in jail.
> STUDENT B: Please don't put me in jail!

1. manager / little girl / (−) to cry
2. cashier / Mrs. Brown / to wait a minute
3. Mrs. Philips / the others / to get out of the way
4. Miss Morales / Mr. Chen / to pick up her packages
5. Mrs. Grant / Mr. Jones / (−) to put the contracts in the drawer
6. the president / them / to have a seat
7. Mr. Conroy / the children / (−) to play with the toys
8. James / the salesman / to show him a camera
9. the saleswoman / her boss / to give her another chance
10. Concepcion / Raul / to speak louder
11. Mrs. Nelson / Mr. Harris / to call an ambulance
12. I / you / (−) to discuss the matter with anyone else

B. Use indirect commands. Use *told* when the person does not say "please"; use *asked* when the person says "please."

"Give me a report later, Bob," Mr. Powell said.
Mr. Powell told Bob to give him a report later.

1. "Put your hands up!" the thief said to the bank clerk.
2. "Please take a message, Ms. Baker," the manager said.
3. "Let me know the answer as soon as possible," Mrs. Rich said to the personnel manager.
4. "Meet me at the service station," Joan said to Bill.
5. "John, please type those reports," Mr. Brown said.
6. "Please give me a chance, Mrs. Rich," Jerry said.
7. "Please fill out some forms," the receptionist said to Bob.
8. "Check the orders, Mrs. Fitzgerald," the boss said.
9. "Terry, please make the deposit immediately," the bank manager said.
10. "Please clean the carburetor," the mechanic said to Mike.
11. "Jerry, put the typewriter on my desk," Mrs. Johnson said.
12. "Please give me all the details," the marketing manager said to Bob.

Grammar Summary

1. Indirect Objects and Indirect Object Pronouns

In the sentence *Mrs. Rich gave her boss the reports* there are both a direct object *(the reports)* and an indirect object *(her boss)*. Indirect object pronouns are the same as direct object pronouns:

> When she saw **him** *(direct)* she gave **him** *(indirect)* the reports *(direct)*.
> She loves **me** *(direct)*, but she won't tell **me** *(indirect)* anything *(direct)*.
> I sent **them** *(indirect)* the contracts *(direct)*, but they lost **them** *(direct)*.
> He hired **us** *(direct)*, but he never gave **us** *(indirect)* a chance *(direct)* to learn.

2. Indirect Commands

"Please do it as quickly as possible," he said to me. He **asked me to do** it as quickly as possible.
"Please don't play your guitar," he said to me. He **asked me not to play** my guitar.
"Comb your hair, Bob!" his mother said. Bob's mother **told him to comb** his hair.
"Don't use my comb!" Bob's mother said. Bob's mother **told him not to use** her comb.
"Please tell Mrs. Grant to go home and not to worry," the doctor said to the nurse. Then the nurse said to Mrs. Grant, "Dr. Smith **asked me to tell** you to go home and not to worry."

NOTE: There is always an indirect object and any possessive adjectives must change: *Bob's mother told **him** not to use **her** comb.* Note, too, that in negative infinitives, the *not* comes before the *to*: **not to play** my guitar, **not to use** her comb, **not to worry.**

3. Reported Speech

We use reported speech to tell what another person said:

NOTE: Sometimes we use *that: Dr. Smith says (that) you'll be all right; She says (that) she doesn't know.*

DEVELOPING YOUR SKILLS

A. Make indirect commands. Use *told* or *asked*.

Peter to John: Close the door!   *Peter told John to close the door.*

1. Mrs. Spencer to her secretary: "Don't use my telephone!"
2. Mr. Jones to Mrs. Rich: "Call me again later."

3. Mr. Schmidt to Mr. Turner's secretary: "Please give Mr. Turner a message."
4. Bill to Mike: "You must send their order immediately."
5. Raul to Yoko: "Please lend me your tent."
6. Mrs. Harris to her husband: "Don't wait for me."
7. Mrs. Rich to me: "Please come back this afternoon."
8. Mr. Moore to us: "You mustn't talk when other people are talking."

B. Use indirect statements.

1. "I'm terribly sorry. It won't happen again." (she says)
2. "I'm just waiting for the report." (he says)
3. "I know Jerry was in London yesterday." (she says)
4. "I think it's going to be a difficult matter to solve." (he says)
5. "We weren't able to get the contracts." (they say)
6. "I guess she's going to give us a chance." (he says)
7. "The cost of living will stay the same." (the president promises)
8. "We hope the prices won't go up this year." (they say)

Reading 1

TENDERBEEF CANNING COMPANY
Pinetown, Colorado 00039

September 3, 1983

Manager
Brown and Walker Ltd.
201 High Street
Manchester,
England

Dear Sir:

I'm traveling to Germany for the Cologne Food Fair next month. After the fair I intend to spend some time with our agents* in Germany, France, and England. I would like to meet either you or someone from your marketing department to discuss the price of our products for next year. I will be in London from November 2 to 5 and will be able to travel to Manchester on the 4th. Could you arrange an appointment for that afternoon? Please let me know if the time and date are convenient for you.

Yours truly,

Steve Parker

Steven Parker
Sales Manager

---

*Here, *agents* = *salesmen and saleswomen.*

Ask Mr. Parker: 1. why he's traveling to Germany next month.   2. what he intends to do after the fair.   3. who he would like to meet in England.   4. when he will be in London.   5. what date will be most convenient for him.

Reading 2

BROWN & WALKER LTD.
201, High Street, Manchester

16th September 1983

```
Mr. Steven Parker
Sales Manager,
Tenderbeef Canning Company,
68 Maple Road,
Pinetown, Colorado   00039
U.S.A.

Dear Mr. Parker,

Thank you for your letter of September 3.  We will be happy to have you with
us on November 4.  Unfortunately I won't be able to see you myself because I
will be in Birmingham for a sales meeting.  I have asked Mr. Potter, our
marketing manager, to meet you at 2 P.M.  He has got* a lot of experience
and will be able to help you in whatever you need.

Yours faithfully,
```

James Wilcox

```
James Wilcox
Manager
```

About Reading 2

1. Why is Mr. Wilcox thanking Mr. Parker?   2. Why won't Mr. Wilcox be able to see Mr. Parker?   3. Who is Mr. Potter?   4. What has Mr. Wilcox asked Mr. Potter to do?   5. Has Mr. Potter worked in marketing for a long time? 6. Do you have a lot of experience in anything? What?

Talk About Yourself

1. Are you usually on time? What do you do when you are not on time?   2. Have you ever been late for a date or an important appointment? What happened?   3. Have you ever forgotten to give somebody a message? What happened?   4. Have you ever signed a contract? What for?   5. Do you have to write / type reports in your job? What kinds? Do you type well?   6. Do any industries have fairs in your country? Which ones?

*Has got (British) = has (American).

George got the following message from Kiku. Write it correctly. (2 points each sentence)

TELL ANN MEET ME AIRPORT GATE 5 ASK BRING MY GUN TELL MUSTN'T TALK
ANYONE TELL HER I SAY NOT TELL POLICE MY PARENTS TELL HER I SAY URGENT
AND MUST BE ON TIME.

KIKU

Total Score _____

LESSON 6

CONVERSATION 1

HIJACKER: This is a hijacking. I have a bomb, so just
do as I say. I want you to return to Utopia
immediately. And don't try anything funny.[1]
If you do, I'll blow up this plane.

5 CAPTAIN: All right, all right. You don't have to shout.
We aren't deaf.

HIJACKER: Now look here, smart guy. Just shut up or I'll
kill you. *(He goes to speak to the passengers.)*
Pay attention, everybody. I have a bomb in this
10 box. If I pull this string, . . . BOOM! Now don't
be frightened. Nobody's going to get hurt if you
do what I tell you. If not, then it'll be all over.

CONVERSATION 2

MR. BOLT: Hello. This is the president of Moronia Airlines.

HIJACKER: Now listen to me carefully. I want you to tell the
Arabs to reduce the price of oil, the Brazilians
to reduce the price of coffee, and the French to
5 reduce the price of wine. Unless they do that I'm
going to blow up this plane. You have until
tomorrow evening at 6:00.

MR. BOLT: And if they can't?

HIJACKER: Either they do or else[2] . . .

CONVERSATION 3

MR. O'LEARY: Look! He's asleep. And he isn't holding the
string anymore. Listen. I'll throw myself
on him and you get the bomb. I'll worry
about the gun.[3]

5 MS. N'KOMO: What will we do if he wakes up?

MR. O'LEARY: Just pray. Are you ready?

MS. N'KOMO: I guess so.

---

[1]Don't try anything funny. = Don't try to stop me.
[2]Either they do or else. = If they don't, I'll blow up the plane.
[3]I'll worry about the gun. = Don't worry about the gun; I'll get it.

New Words

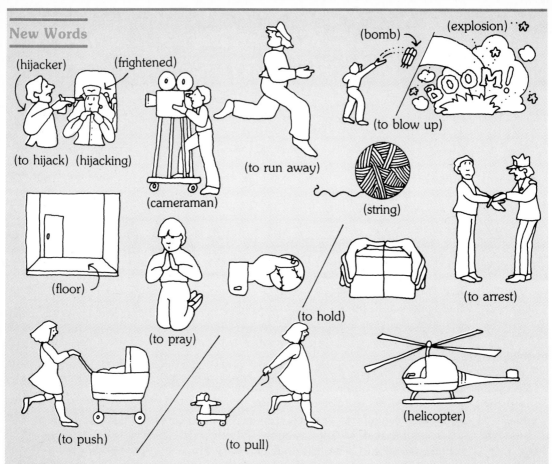

(hijacker) (frightened) (bomb) (explosion)

(to hijack) (hijacking) (to blow up)

(cameraman) (to run away)

(string)

(floor) (to hold) (to arrest)

(to pray)

(to push) (to pull) (helicopter)

DEFINITIONS

Arab: person from North Africa, Saudi Arabia, Syria, etc.

all over: *(adj.)* when you have finished something, it is all over; *(adv.)* everywhere.

to belong: when something is yours, it belongs to you.

by: *here:* before; not later than: *I need your report by this afternoon.*

deaf: not able to hear.

do as I say: do what I tell you to do.

to get hurt: to hurt yourself while you are doing something; to be hurt because of an accident.

guy: *(colloquial)* man; boy.

listen here / look here: We use these expressions when we are angry (usually with children); they mean *listen! / look!*

neither . . . nor: not one and not the other: *Neither Bill nor Bob ran away.*

or else: do as I say or something bad will happen.

passenger: person who is traveling on a plane, train, etc.; people besides the driver who are traveling in a car: *Four people died in the accident—the driver and three passengers.*

to pay attention: to listen or watch very carefully.

to reduce: to make something lower or less in price, number, size, etc.

Shut up!: *(not nice)* don't talk!

smart guy: *(not nice)* We use this expression to speak to someone who is not doing what we said to do.

Thank goodness!: We use this expression when we are very glad something happened.

unless: if not: *Unless they reduce the price, I won't buy it.* = *If they don't reduce the price, I won't buy it.*

until: *(prep.)* from now to another time: *I'll stay here until Sunday; (conj.)* from now to the time something happens: *I won't return until they arrest him.*

Whew!: We use this expression when we are glad something is not happening anymore or when we have finished a hard job.

MINI-CONVERSATION 1

A: Look, why don't you buy this camera? It takes excellent photographs, and if you don't like it, just bring it back.

B: The problem is that neither my wife nor I have much experience with cameras. So we won't be able to use it right.

A: I'll show you, unless you're in a hurry.

MINI-CONVERSATION 2

A: Wilkins? This is Ted Collins at Smith & Jones. If we don't get our order soon we're going to be in trouble.

B: I didn't know it was urgent.

A: Now listen here, Wilkins. Either you send us that order by this afternoon or else.

CONVERSATION PRACTICE

About Conversation 1

1. What does the hijacker want the captain to do?   2. What will he do if the captain doesn't do as he says?   3. What does the captain tell the hijacker not to do?   4. What will the hijacker do if the captain isn't quiet?   5. What will happen if the passengers do as he tells them? What will happen if they don't?

About Conversation 2

1. Who is the hijacker talking to?   2. What does he want Mr. Bolt to do?   3. Why do you think the hijacker wants the Arabs, the Brazilians, and the French to reduce their prices?
4. What will happen to the passengers? What will happen to the hijacker?   5. How long does the president have to solve the problem?

About Conversation 3

1. What isn't the hijacker holding anymore?   2. What does Mr. O'Leary want to do?   3. What must Ms. N'Komo do?   4. What do you think will happen?

Situation 1

You are very angry because something you've been waiting for hasn't arrived. Call the store, bank, person, etc., and complain. If this thing doesn't arrive, you will . . .

Situation 2

You are trying to sell somebody something. If the person buys it, he / she will . . .

Situation 3

Ask someone to marry you. Tell all of the things you will / won't do if he / she marries you.

SUMMARY OF NEW WORDS

VERBS: REGULAR

to arrest / arrested / arrested
to belong / belonged / belonged
to hijack / hijacked / hijacked

to pray / prayed / prayed
to pull / pulled / pulled

to push / pushed / pushed
to reduce / reduced / reduced

VERBS: IRREGULAR

to blow up / blew up / blown up   to hold / held / held   to run away / ran away / run away

NOUNS

Arab(s)   cameraman (men)   floor(s)   helicopter(s)   hijacking(s)   string(s)
bomb(s)   explosion(s)   guy(s)   hijacker(s)   passenger(s)

ADJECTIVES   CONJUNCTIONS

all over   deaf   frightened   neither . . . nor   unless   until

PREPOSITIONS   PHRASES AND EXPRESSIONS

by + *time*   Boom!   listen / look here!   Shut up!   Thank goodness!
until   do as I say   or else   smart guy   Whew!
                  to get hurt   to pay attention

EXERCISES

A. Use Cue Book Chart 5. Start with *there's / fire / **1** / try to stop it.*

   If there's a fire, the firefighters will try to stop it.

1. hijacker / leave / plane / **2** / arrest him
2. there's / explosion / **3** / write a great story
3. somebody / get hurt / **4** / take him to the hospital
4. there's / explosion / **5** / turn on the camera
5. plane / blow up / all of the / **6** / die
6. hijacker / see / **7** / pull the string
7. passengers / die / **8** / be very sorry
8. plane / blow up / **9** / be able to hear the explosion
9. there's / explosion / **10** / be able to see it
10. plane / blow up / **1** / may die too

B. Use Cue Book Chart 5. Answer the questions.

1. Is the airport busy today? Why?
2. Is it far from the city? Is that good or bad? Why?
3. Why can't the planes on the ground take off?
4. Why are they taking food to the plane?
5. Which newspaper do the reporters work at?
6. What are the soldiers on top of the plane going to do?
7. There is a man who is bringing food. How does he feel?
8. How many planes are waiting to land? What will they do if they can't?
9. Why is the gas truck far from the plane?

Grammar Summary

1. Conditional (Type 1): If / When; If Not / Unless / Either . . . Or

If or *when* something happens, something else will happen:

> You'll be very happy **if / when** you marry me.
> Will you marry me **if** I buy you a diamond ring?

NOTE: We use the simple present (*not* the future) after *if* and *when: I'll push the car **if it breaks down;** I'll be happy **when you come back.***

If something does *not* happen or *unless* it happens, something else will happen:

> **If** you **don't** come ⎫
> **Unless** you come ⎭ I won't talk to you again.

We can also use *either . . . or* to describe this:

> **Either** you come ⎰ **or** I won't talk to you again.
> ⎱ **or else.**

2. Conjunctions: Either . . . Or / Neither . . . Nor

> I'll finish these reports. If I don't, Peter will.
> **Either** Peter **or** I will finish these reports.

> I'm not taking photographs. My wife isn't either.
> **Neither** my wife **nor** I are taking photographs.

We usually use a plural verb after *either . . . or / neither . . . nor*. But remember: When they are used as pronouns, the verb is always singular: ***Either of them is able*** to do the job. ***Neither of us wants*** to take photographs.

NOTE: When we use a 1 singular pronoun *(I, me, my)* with other pronouns, the 1 singular pronoun comes last: *Either he or I . . .; They saw her and me . . .*

DEVELOPING YOUR SKILLS

Use the conjunction to combine the following sentences. Remember to make the sentence affirmative when you have to.

1. Don't play with the bomb, Charlie! You'll kill yourself. (if)
2. The police officer won't be able to arrest the hijacker. He doesn't have a gun. (unless)
3. I wasn't frightened when I heard the explosion. Ted wasn't either. (neither . . . nor)
4. She doesn't understand English. Perhaps she's deaf. (either . . . or)
5. I'm going to Paris on business. I'll come and see you. (when)
6. Pray! Maybe something good will happen. (if)
7. The stores must reduce their prices. Our marketing manager will have to talk to them. (if not)
8. The president didn't want to discuss the matter. The prime minister didn't either. (neither . . . nor)
9. Will you call me later? I'll try to see you after work. (if)
10. Johnny, stop pulling your sister's hair! If you don't, I'll hit you. (either . . . or)

Reading

Good evening, ladies and gentlemen. This is Bob Smith for Channel 9 news. A man who had only a toy gun and an empty chocolate box hijacked a Moronia Airlines plane early this morning. The hijacker, Julian Adams, belonged to the Consumers' Liberation Movement. He wanted the Arabs to
5 reduce the price of oil, the Brazilians the price of coffee, and the French the price of wine.

Neither we nor the police have ever heard of this "movement," but our reporters found out that last week Adams was in Utopia City Hospital for treatment and ran away two days before the hijacking. Two passengers, Mr.
10 Bruce O'Leary and Ms. Elizabeth N'Komo, were able to stop him late this afternoon. Fortunately, nobody got hurt. The police have arrested Adams and taken him back to the hospital. And now for the latest report, here is Tessa Gordon at the airport.

TESSA GORDON: Now some of the passengers who were on this morning's
15   flight will tell us what happened.

MRS. DAPHNE WARD OF BRIGHTON, ENGLAND

I was writing a post card to my daughter when suddenly I heard someone shout. I looked up and saw a man who was holding a gun in one hand and a box in the other. He was telling everybody to sit down and listen. I wasn't able to hear what he was saying very well—you see, I'm a little deaf—but I guessed what it was. I wasn't really frightened, because when you're my
5 age you don't worry about anything anymore, and I didn't think the man looked dangerous at all. In fact, he looked more frightened than we did. I'm glad nobody was hurt and it's all over, but what about that poor man? They say he has a wife and four children. What a shame!

About Mrs. Ward

1. What happened while she was writing the post card?   2. Could she hear what the man was saying? Why?   3. Was she frightened? Why?   4. What did she think of the man?   5. How does she feel now?

MR. NARENDRA GHANDI OF CALCUTTA, INDIA

I was leaving the rest room[1] when I saw him. He was standing with his back to me. For a minute I thought I could jump on him and hold him, but when I saw that bomb in his hand I went back to my seat, sat down, and prayed. Thank goodness my family and I are safe, but I think they should kill these crazy people. Jail is too good for them. If they kill one or two
5   hijackers, others will think before they try to hijack a plane.

About Mr. Ghandi

1. What did Mr. Ghandi think he could do?   2. What did he do when he saw the bomb?   3. Was Mr. Ghandi traveling alone? How do you know?   4. What does he think they should do to hijackers?   5. What does he think will happen if they do that?

MR. BRUCE O'LEARY OF PERTH, AUSTRALIA

Well, I don't know why I did it, but it was really an experience.[2] He was standing next to us, and both Ms. N'Komo and I saw that he was getting sleepy. He was closing his eyes all the time and then quickly opening them. So the first chance we got I threw myself on him. I weigh 250 pounds,[3] you know, so the guy didn't know what hit him.[4] I got his gun, and fortunately the box
5   fell near Elizabeth . . . Ms. N'Komo. She had the hardest job. I just had to sit on the hijacker. She had to hold that box! Of course it was empty, but none of us knew that then.

About Mr. O'Leary

Ask Mr. O'Leary questions about his experience.

MS. ELIZABETH N'KOMO OF NAIROBI, KENYA

Whew! I'm so glad it's all over now. I've never been so frightened in my life. When Mr. O'Leary jumped on him and he dropped that box, I thought it was going to blow up. I felt hot and cold at the same time, but I knew I had to do something. I picked it up, ran to the door, and threw it as far as I could. Then I threw myself on the floor and waited for the explosion. I lay
5   there, but nothing happened. The box was empty. When I think about it now I just want to laugh.

---

[1]Rest room = room with a toilet and sink.
[2]*Here,* experience = something that happened to you.
[3]One pound = 0.454 kilos.
[4]What hit him = what happened to him.

⌐k Ms. N'Komo questions about what happened and how she felt.

Writing

You were on the plane. Use the reading to write about your own experience.

Talk About Yourself

1. Have you ever been in a hijacking? Do you know anyone who has?   2. What do you think they should do to try to stop hijackings?   3. Have you ever been really frightened? When? Talk about it.   4. Have you ever seen an explosion? What kind? Talk about it.

Test Yourself

Write the following sentences in four different ways. (½ point each)

They should arrest him. He'll run away.

> If they arrest him he won't run away.
> If they don't arrest him he'll run away.
> Unless they arrest him he'll run away.
> Either they arrest him or he'll run away.

1. The firefighters must stop the fire. The plane will blow up.
2. You have to pay attention. You won't understand what I'm saying.
3. They should tell him to stop. He'll get hurt.
4. We must leave quickly. We won't arrive on time.
5. They have to hold their children. There won't be enough seats.

Total Score _____

What to say . . .

Song WILL YOU MARRY ME?

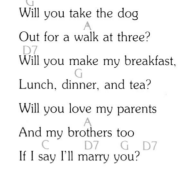

G
Will you wash the windows?
A
Will you feed the cat?
D7
Will you change the tire
G
When I have a flat?
5 Will you do the things
A
That I ask you to
C   D7 G   D7
If I say I'll marry you?

G
I'll fix the roof and the door
I'll fix the hole in the floor
A
10 We'll be a happy family
D7
I'll take the kids for a drive
Teach them to swim and to dive
C   D7 G   D7
If you say you'll marry me.

G
Will you take the dog
A
15 Out for a walk at three?
D7
Will you make my breakfast,
G
Lunch, dinner, and tea?
Will you love my parents
A
And my brothers too
C   D7   G   D7
20 If I say I'll marry you?

G
I'll bring you breakfast in bed—
A cup of tea, eggs, and bread—
A
I'll watch your programs on TV
D7
I'll keep your feet warm at night
25 I'll make everything all right
C   D7   G   D7
If you say you'll marry me.

G   A
Will you think of me when you're far away?
D7
Will you write me?
G
Will you call me every day?
30 Will you scratch my back?
A
Will you cure my flu
C   D7   G   D7
If I say I'll marry you?

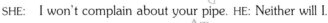

G
SHE: I won't complain about your pipe. HE: Neither will I.
                    Am
HE: I'll never smoke in bed at night. SHE: Neither will I.
                    D7
35 SHE: I'll never shout if there's a fight. HE: Neither will I.
                    G   E♭7
HE: I'll read the poetry that you write. SHE: So will I.
                    A♭
SHE: I'll travel with you everywhere. HE: So will I.
                    B♭m
HE: I'll miss you so when you aren't there. SHE: So will I.
                    E♭7
SHE: I think that both of us are fair. HE: So do I.
                    A♭
40 BOTH: I know we'll make a perfect pair. EVERYONE: So do we.

LESSON 7

CONVERSATION

ANN: Hello, Mary. Is it true you're going to leave us?

MARY: Maybe, but it still depends on Jack's interview. If he gets that job, then we'll have to move to Boswell.

ANN: You're going to miss Highland Park, aren't you?

5 MARY: Oh, definitely. But it's a much greater opportunity for Jack. His salary will be higher and he'll have a much better position. He'll manage the whole sales department. Also, there are better schools for the children. The town itself isn't half as nice as Highland Park, of course.

ANN: Yes, there are so many factories. There's probably a lot of air pollution, isn't there?

10 MARY: Yes, and not much green area either. But that's life, I guess.

ANN: Are you going to stop working?

MARY: I believe I'll have to at first, but I intend to go back to work as soon as we settle down. I may get a job teaching.* There's a new high school there and they're looking for teachers.

15 ANN: Have you decided what you're going to do with your house here?

MARY: Well, we were thinking of selling it and buying a new one in Boswell. But we can't make up our minds. Houses are expensive there, so we may just rent one.

ANN: It'll be a shame if you have to sell it. You've fixed it up so nicely.

MARY: You know, Ann, deep down I really don't want to move. I know it's for the best, but I'm
20 not sure I can get used to living in a town as big as Boswell. I've lived in small towns all my life.

ANN: Of course you can. You may not like it at first, but you'll get used to it. And besides, you and Jack are the kind of people who make friends easily. I'm sure you'll be very happy there, and I wish you the best of luck. You deserve it!

25 MARY: You're very sweet, Ann. You and Bob must come to see us if we move.

---

*NOTE: We use the present participle (-ing form) to describe a job: *He has a job washing windows; I hope to find a job arranging tours.*

I speak English.
He/she speaks
English.

(to teach)

(air pollution)

(water pollution)

DEFINITIONS

at first: when you start.

to be / get used to: when you do / see / hear, etc., something often enough you get used to it.

to believe: to think; to be sure.

to decide: to know what you want to do or what you or someone else should do (usually after you have thought about it or discussed it).

deep: far down.

deep down (*or:* **down deep**): in your heart. We use this expression to describe how someone really feels about something.

definitely: certainly; without any question.

to deserve: to get what you should get: *If you do good work, you deserve a good salary.*

to feel like + -ing: to want to do.

to fix up: to make something pretty or nice.

for the best / worst: it's the best / worst thing.

to go back to work: to return to your job after a vacation or after you have been sick; to get a new job after you have left another one.

interview: meeting where one or more people ask questions to try to learn about someone or something. When you apply for a job you usually have interviews with the personnel department and with the person who will be your boss.

to make friends: to get new friends.

to make up your mind: to decide.

to manage: to be the boss of a business or a department.

to move: to change something's place (*He moved the couch*); to change the place where you live (*I moved to a new apartment*). NOTE: **to move around:** to move something or to go from one place to another very often.

not half as . . . as: much less . . . than: *Boswell isn't half as nice as Highland Park.* = *Highland Park is much nicer than Boswell.*

opportunity: chance.

position: job.

to settle (down): to arrange things so you can be quiet and comfortable.

sweet: not sour; kind: *Sugar is sweet and so are you.*

to think of doing: to plan to do.

true: right; what really happened, is happening, or will happen.

CONVERSATION 1

o you feel like going out tonight?

don't know really. How about you?

A: Well, I was thinking of going to the races. Do you want to?

B: I may, but what will we do with the kids?

A: We can leave them with my mother.

MINI-CONVERSATION 2

A: Dad, I'm going to look for another job.

B: You're what?! You should stop moving around and try to settle down.

A: I've tried to, but I'll never get used to working in a factory.

B: Of course you will. It's a wonderful opportunity. Someday you may get a very good position there.

A: That may be true, but I hate working there.

B: Just make up your mind to enjoy it and I know you'll be able to.

CONVERSATION PRACTICE

About the Conversation

1. Is Mary definitely moving to Boswell? Why?   2. What kind of job will Jack have?   3. What's Boswell like?   4. Is Mary going to stop working? Until when?   5. What kind of job will she probably get?   6. What do they intend to do with their house? Have they decided yet? Why?   7. Why doesn't Mary want to move to Boswell?   8. What does Ann think about that?   9. What do Mary and Jack deserve?   10. What does Mary say that Ann and Bob will have to do?

Situation 1

You are telling a friend why he / she shouldn't go camping alone. It's too dangerous because of . . . and he / she may . . . , etc.

Situation 2

You are telling a friend not to go somewhere on vacation because . . . Describe the place and say what may or may not happen there.

Situation 3

You have lost your job. Tell a friend what you may do now. (Perhaps you plan to start your own business. Say what kind, how you intend to start it, etc.)

SUMMARY OF NEW WORDS

VERBS: REGULAR

to believe / believed / believed	to manage / managed / managed
to decide / decided / decided	to move / moved / moved
to deserve / deserved / deserved	to settle (down) / settled / settled

VERBS: IRREGULAR	ADJECTIVES			ADVERBS		
to teach / taught / taught	deep	sweet	true	at first	definitely	nicely

NOUNS

interview(s)   opportunity (opportunities)   pollution   position(s)

PHRASES AND EXPRESSIONS

to be / get used to + -ing	to fix up	to make up (your) mind(s)
deep down	for the best / worst	not half as . . . as
to do with	to go back to work	to think of + -ing
to feel like + -ing	to make friends	

EXERCISES

A. Say. Use Cue Book Chart 5. Start with **10** / (−)*be able* / *land*.

The planes may not be able to land.

1. **1** / (−)be able / stop / fire
2. **2** / arrest / hijacker
3. **3** / (−)have / interviews
4. **4** / have to take / people / hospital
5. **5** / have to move out of the way

6. **6** / get hurt
7. **7** / have / opportunity / go inside
8. **8** / (−)believe / it / be / very serious matter
9. **9** / hear / explosion
10. **10** / decide / go / another airport

B. Use the right word or expression to answer.

1. A: What did they do with their house when they moved?
   B: *(They fixed it up and sold it. / They settled down there and just loved it.)*
2. A: Please! Just give me one more chance.
   B: *(I've taught you everything I know. / You've had all the opportunities you deserve.)*
3. A: I don't believe I'll ever get used to this air pollution. Whose fault is it?
   B: *(It's because of all the industries nearby. / It's all the green areas.)*
4. A: Have you had your interview yet?
   B: *(Yes, but there were no positions available. / I believe so.)*
5. A: Have they decided definitely when they're going to move?
   B: *(Yes, the first of June. / At first they couldn't make up their minds.)*
6. A: Do you feel like going back to work yet?
   B: *(No, I'm not half as sick as I was. / Actually, deep down I don't ever want to.)*
7. A: Didn't you use to manage the Dove's Inn?
   B: *(Yes, I worked there for many years. / Yes, I used to think of being a manager someday.)*
8. A: They say that everything's always for the best.
   B: *(I guess that's true. / That's very sweet of you.)*

Auxiliary Verb May = Maybe

Sometimes when we use *may* it means *maybe* or *perhaps:*

A: Is it going to rain?

B: { It may.   It may not.
   { Maybe (it will).   Maybe not. / Maybe it won't.

A: Do you know if they're coming?

B: { They may.   They may not.
   { Maybe (they will). Maybe not. / Maybe they won't.

NOTE: We ask questions with *may* only when we're asking permission: **May I come in? May we borrow your vacuum cleaner?**

2. There Is / There Are *with Auxiliary Verbs*

We use *there is* and *there are* in all tenses and with auxiliary verbs: For example:

There may be a party tonight. **There used to be** parties every night, but **there haven't been** any for a long time. **There weren't** any last week and I don't believe **there'll be** any next week. **There can't be** a party tomorrow night and **there aren't going to be** any this weekend. What a boring life! **There have to be** parties sometimes, **don't there?**

3. Verb + Infinitive: Short Form

We use infinitives after many verbs: *be able, decide, hate, like, love, need, plan, refuse, try, want,* etc. We also use *to* with some auxiliary verbs: *going to, have to, use(d) to.* We usually think of the *to* as belonging to the verb that comes before it. Note the short form:

Why are you moving?   Because I **have to** (move).
Have they fixed up their office yet?   No, but they're **going to** (fix it up).
Do you believe everything they say?   No, but I **used to** (believe everything they say).
Have you apologized?   No, and I don't **intend to** (apologize).
Will you have an interview soon?   I **hope to** (have an interview soon).

4. Verb + Present Participle

Some verbs and expressions use a present participle (*-ing* form) after them:

to enjoy: I **enjoy managing** this supermarket.
to finish: We haven't **finished discussing** the problem yet.
to stop: Please **stop smoking.**
to be / get used to: I'll never **get used to getting up** so early.
to feel like: I **feel like taking** a hot shower.
to have trouble: You'll never **have trouble finding** a job.
to think of: We're **thinking of settling** down here.

These verbs can have either an infinitive or a participle:

to begin: Suddenly he **began to sing** / **began singing.**

to start: When I told the joke they all **started to laugh** / **started laughing.**

to like / to prefer: She **likes** / **prefers to walk** / **likes** / **prefers walking.**

NOTE: When the verb *to stop* has an infinitive after it, it means one thing; when it has a present participle after it, it means something else:

I **stopped praying.** = I was praying and then I stopped.

I **stopped to pray.** = I was doing something and then I stopped and began to pray.

DEVELOPING YOUR SKILLS

A. What do you think is inside the package? Write six sentences. It may be . . .

B. Answer the questions *ad lib.*, using one of the following verbs + the short form of the infinitive. (Don't use the same verb more than two times.)

to be able	going to	to hope	to love	to promise	to try
to begin	to hate	to intend	to need	to refuse	use(d) to
to forget	to have to	to like	to plan	to start	to want

1. Why don't you help yourself?
2. Are you going to use this recipe?
3. Do you ever use make-up anymore?
4. Would you like to go sailing?
5. Why didn't he spend any money?
6. Didn't he take the message?
7. Do they get frightened at night?
8. Did he ever surf?
9. Why aren't they laughing?
10. Is he going back to work?
11. Why don't you pay attention?
12. Why didn't they arrest him?
13. Will they fix the radiator?
14. Did you check the oil?

C. Billy Hick is from the country, but now he's living in a big town. What will he have to get used to?

He'll have to get used to the subway.
He'll have to get used to going on the subway.

Write four sentences using nouns and four sentences using verbs. Then tell what he will *enjoy* in the city. Again, write four sentences using nouns and four sentences using verbs.

1. Talk about the things that you can't get used to. 2. Talk about the things that you have gotten used to. 3. Would you like to move to a different house / apartment / town / country? Why? 4. Do you have trouble getting used to living in a different town / country? 5. If you have moved from your hometown, what do you miss the most? 6. Is there much pollution where you live? Whose fault is it? 7. Do you want to move from your town / country or have you settled down? 8. Do you prefer to live in a small town or a big town? Why?

Test Yourself

Make sentences. Use Cue Book Chart 1. Start with **8** / (−)*find stairs.* (1 point each)

He may not find the stairs.

1. **9** / (−)like / color
2. **10** / exchange / sweater
3. **11** / (−)listen to him
4. **12** / buy / expensive / camera
5. **13** / (−)choose / latest hit

6. **15** / (−)be able / hear
7. **16** / have to go / hospital
8. **17** / (−)buy anything
9. **18** / believe / too expensive
10. **19** / decide / to try on

Total Score _____

What to say. . .

LESSON 8

CONVERSATION

Carol Ives is interviewing Tony Wilkins, star of the Springfield soccer team.

CAROL: Now, Tony, what do you like best about being a soccer star?

TONY: Well, I love to hear the cheering when I'm playing, especially when I score a goal. And I enjoy meeting people, but I always feel embarrassed when they ask me for my autograph. I guess
5   I'm shy. And, of course, the pay is good.

CAROL: Do you get nervous?

TONY: Before the game, yes, but not during it.

CAROL: Can you tell us something about your training?

TONY: Well, we train very hard, especially before a big[1] game.
10   The team has to stay together on the road—sometimes for weeks—and I find[2] that very boring.

CAROL: Are you worried about tomorrow's game?[3]

TONY: No. Even if we lose we'll probably still get the cup. You see, we've scored more goals than Northern City,
15   so they'll have to win by at least four goals if they want the cup. I don't think they can do it.

CAROL: Thank you, Tony, and good luck tomorrow.

● ● ●

CAROL: Hello, folks. This morning I talked to Tony Wilkins, star of the Springfield soccer team. I asked Tony what he liked most about his job. He said he loved to hear the cheering
20 crowds. He said he enjoyed meeting people, but he felt[4] that signing autographs was very embarrassing. Tony told me the pay was good. I believe his salary is over a million Q a year now, so he should be able to save a little for the future. When I asked him if he ever got nervous, he said he did, but never during a game. I then asked him to talk about the training he does. He said he trained very hard, especially before an important
25 game, but he found being on the road very boring. When I asked him about tomorrow's game he said he wasn't especially worried because Northern City wouldn't get the cup unless they won by four goals. Tony didn't think they could do it. And I really don't either.

---

[1]Here, *big = important.*
[2]Here, *to find = to think that.*
[3]NOTE: the game tomorrow = tomorrow's game; the weather this morning = this morning's weather, etc.
[4]Here, *to feel = to believe.*

New Words

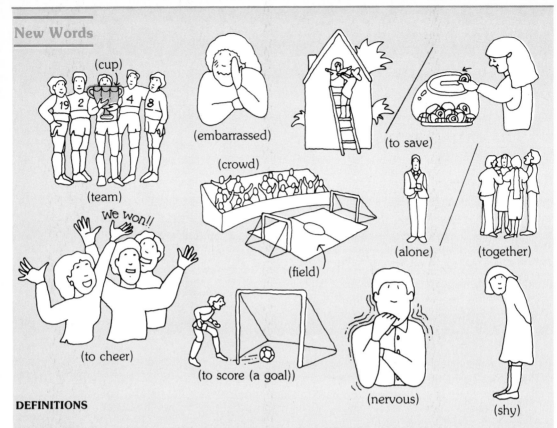

(cup)

(team)

(embarrassed)

(crowd)

(to save)

(alone)

(together)

We won!!

(to cheer)

(field)

(to score (a goal))

(nervous)

(shy)

DEFINITIONS

to ask for: to ask if you can have something; to ask if you can speak to someone: *She asked for the champion, and when he arrived she asked him for his autograph.*

at least: not less than.

autograph: when a famous person signs his or her name for someone.

coach: person who manages a sports team, tells the players when and how to train, how to play, etc.

condition: when someone is healthy or something is not broken, he / she / it is in good condition; when they are not healthy or are broken, they are in bad (or poor) condition.

embarrassing: a person is embarrassed when something embarrassing happens.

especially: more than usually.

to feel (that): to believe (that).

to find (that): to think (that).

hour (day, week, etc.) after hour (day, week, etc.): for a long time without changing or stopping.

to interview: to have an interview.

on the road: traveling.

pay: money you get for your work; salary.

sports: soccer, tennis, golf, etc.

to train: to work hard and get ready for a game.

MINI-CONVERSATION 1

A: Where's Sophia?
B: She isn't here.
A: Did she say what time she'd be back?
B: No. She just said she had a doctor's appointment and that she was going to be late.
A: Well, when she comes back, tell her I asked for her.

MINI-CONVERSATION 2

A: Is the engine in good condition?
B: Yes, it is.
A: And can Charlie fix the radiator?
B: He said he could.
A: Terrific! When will he do it?
B: He said he'd do it after lunch.
A: Fine.

MINI-CONVERSATION 3

A: Who does the coach think is going to win?
B: He says the winning team will be the one that scores the first goal.
A: Why does he say that?
B: Because the losing team usually gets nervous and their* playing becomes careless.
A: Well, good luck! I hope you score first.

CONVERSATION PRACTICE

About the Conversation

1. What does Tony like to hear when he scores a goal?   2. Does he get nervous during the game? When does he get nervous?   3. What does he say about the pay?   4. What does he say about giving autographs?   5. What does he say about training before a big game?
6. What does he think about being on the road for a long time?   7. What does he say about the next day's game?   8. Why does he think Springfield will win the cup?

Situation 1

You interviewed a famous person. Tell your friend what he / she said.

Situation 2

Somebody left a message for your boss. Tell him / her what the person said.

Situation 3

You heard an interesting interview on the radio. Tell your friend what the person said.

---

*We call *team* a "collective noun." This means that the word suggests more than one person or thing. So we say "The team *is* good. *They play* very well." Another collective noun you know is *pair*: "My new pair *is* blue, but I'm afraid *they're* dirty."

VERBS: REGULAR

to ask for / asked for / asked for
to cheer / cheered / cheered
to interview / interviewed / interviewed

to save / saved / saved
to score / scored / scored
to train / trained / trained

AUXILIARY VERBS

will / would

NOUNS

autograph(s)   condition(s)   cup(s)   goal(s)   sport(s)
coach(es)   crowd(s)   field(s)   pay   team(s)

ADJECTIVES

embarrassed (by)   embarrassing   nervous   shy

ADVERBS

at least   especially   together

CONJUNCTIONS

together with

PHRASES AND EXPRESSIONS

to feel that   Good luck!   hour after hour (day after day, etc.)   on the road
to find that

EXERCISES

Use the right word or expression.

1. Tony certainly has grown. He's *(at least / especially)* six feet tall now.
2. Interviewers have to enjoy meeting people. They can't be *(embarrassing / shy)*.
3. I spent a fortune to fix up the car because it was *(in very poor condition / on the road)*.
4. I shouted louder than anyone when the team *(cheered / scored)* a goal.
5. She was terribly shy and wouldn't even go to a small party unless she and her husband were *(nervous / together)*.
6. The winning team got an enormous *(crowd / cup)*.
7. We're going to have to play even if the *(coach / field)* is wet.
8. You should *(save / spend)* your money if you want to get rich.
9. When you're a sports star you have to sign a lot of *(autographs / goals)*.
10. The coach was very embarrassed by the present. He felt it was much too *(expensive / shy)*.

Grammar Summary

1. Reported Speech in Present and Past Tenses

Sometimes we use *that*, but we don't have to:

Tony says: "I train very hard." **Tony says (that) he trains** very hard.
Jane says: "I'll meet them at 6:00." **Jane says (that) she'll meet** them at 6:00.

When the main verb *(say / tell)* is in the past tense, the reported verb is often in the past:

> **They said: "We want** an autograph." → **They said (that) they wanted** an autograph.
>
> **He used to say: "My team is** the best." → **He used to say (that) his team was** the best.
>
> **She said: "We can** work together." → **She said (that) they** *(or:* **we) could** work together.
>
> **Mike said: "Joan has to** work late." → **Mike said (that) Joan had to** work late.
>
> **Maria said: "Mr. Cash is going to** play tennis." → **Maria said (that) Mr. Cash was going to** play tennis.
>
> **Raul said: "I'll go** to New York." → **Raul said (that) he would go** to New York.
>
> **Joan said: "I won't ask** for anything." → **Joan said (that) she wouldn't ask** for anything.

NOTE: When the main verb is in the past, *will* → *would.*

If we use *tell,* we must always use an indirect object:

> **Tony told me: "I used to train** very hard." → **Tony told me (that) he used to train** very hard.

2. *Reported Questions: Ask*

Note the word order:

> Tony always asks: "How many goals did you score?" → Tony always **asks how many goals I** *(or:* **we) scored.**
>
> Joan asked: "Why is she cheering?" → Joan **asked why she was cheering.**

When there is no question word, we must use *if:*

> Tony asked me: "Do you like soccer?" → Tony **asked me if I liked** soccer.

3. *Present Participles as Adjectives*

We call the *-ing* form the present participle. We sometimes use this as an adjective.

> The **winning team** gets the cup. (the team that wins)
> Tony loves to hear the **cheering crowds.** (the crowds that cheer)

4. *Present Participles as Nouns*

Sometimes we use present participles as nouns:

> Tony doesn't like **meeting people** and he hates **signing autographs.**
> His **training** is definitely better than ours.

We can also use present participles after prepositions:

> I'm **tired of studying.**
> They talked **about traveling.**

DEVELOPING YOUR SKILLS

A. Use Cue Book Chart 1. Start with **20** / *Mrs. Gomez* / *to be* / *too tight*.

Mrs. Gomez said (that) the boots were too tight.

1. **21** / Mrs. Tanaka / to be / too low
2. **22** / Mr. Olsen / to be / too small
3. **23** / Mary / to be / pleased / to meet him
4. **24** / Mr. Carter / to be / too big
5. **25** / Mr. Ross / to be / sorry
6. **1** / the thief / to be / just looking
7. **2** / the child / his mother / to be / there
8. **3** / Mr. Smith / to be / inexpensive
9. **4** / the cashier / to have / no change
10. **6** / Miss Baker / to be / his fault

B. Use Cue Book Chart 2. Start with **1** / "I love you."

He said (that) he loved her. Or: She said (that) she loved him.

1. **3** / "I'm going to tell my dad."
2. **4** / "We want to take some photographs."
3. **5** / "The bride and groom look terribly shy."
4. **7** / "We won't get home on time."
5. **8** / "He's going to kill that cat."
6. **9** / "The sun is too hot for the baby."
7. **12** / "I'll save you."
8. **14** / "COACH THROWS BOTTLE AT CROWD."
9. **15** / "You're a terrible driver."
10. **17** / "My team is going to score more goals than yours."

C. Use "say" or "tell." Always use the past tense when you can; when you can't, use the present tense.

1. Ann ____ Mary she couldn't save very much because she didn't get a good salary.
2. Mr. Gomez ____ he's going to discuss the matter with his manager.
3. The mechanic ____ he would let us know as soon as it was ready.
4. Mrs. Brook ____ us she was very embarrassed during the reception.
5. Pierre ____ he'll be pleased to check the contracts for you.
6. Carol ____ she interviewed a very interesting person yesterday.
7. Mr. Chen ____ the receptionist the time wasn't very convenient for the meeting.
8. Dr. Barnes ____ he'll come, especially if the matter is urgent.
9. The children ____ they were going to cheer and shout for their team.
10. The prime minister ____ the reporters he prayed that there wouldn't be a war.

D. Use the correct present participle as an adjective or noun in the following sentences:

| to answer | to die | to hire | to make | to save | to visit |
| to cry | to eat | to laugh | to sail | to travel | to welcome |

1. ____ too much between meals is bad for you.
2. ____ on a boat over the deep blue sea is what I like best.
3. I felt that ____ someone who could do the job well wasn't going to be easy.
4. The firefighters had a hard time ____ the man because he was nervous.
5. Before I got this job I used to be a ____ salesman, but I got tired of being on the road.

6. ___ people and ___ the phone is a receptionist's job.
7. ___ is better than ___. That's why I enjoy a good joke.
8. The ___ soldier said that ___ plans just wasn't important anymore.
9. ___ hours at the hospital are from three to four in the afternoon.

Reading

SOCCER: SPECIAL REPORT BY PHIL ROGERS

I spoke to Carlos Rovel, the Springfield coach, at his hotel last night. I asked him if he expected to win tomorrow's game. Carlos told me that his team was in very good condition, that they were playing very well, and that he felt they definitely deserved to win. He said it would be a terrible surprise if they didn't. He knew it was going to be a hard game, but he was looking
5   forward to it. He wasn't worried, and his players weren't especially nervous. I then asked him about the cup. He said they could lose the game and still win the cup, but that was not what he wanted. He told me the team was training at the stadium this afternoon to get used to the field. When I asked him who would play, he said that was a secret, and he would let us know an hour before the game started. He said that sometimes people became too relaxed and careless
10 because they didn't think the team would need them, so he wanted everyone to think that maybe he was going to be a starting player.

Writing

Use the reading to write the conversation between Phil and Carlos. Remember that you will *not* use reported speech in the conversation itself.

Talk About Yourself

1. Do you play soccer? Do you like it? What do / don't you like about soccer?   2. Is soccer popular in your country? Do many people play it or watch it on TV?   3. Are there many teams?
4. Which is your favorite team?   5. Which team won / is going to win the cup this year? Why?
6. Are soccer players very popular in your country? Who's the most popular player? Who do you think is the best player?   7. Do sports players get a lot of money in your country? Should they? Why?   8. What sport do you like best?

Write the following sentences in reported speech. (1 point each)

1. "I enjoy stealing," Buster says.
2. "Did your truck break down, sir?" John asked.
3. "I won't be able to come to the meeting," Jerry told Mrs. Rich.
4. "I'm going to call you and Bob as soon as we get there," Olga said.
5. "I'm afraid I can't give you an interview until after the game," Carlos told Carol.
6. "If you hurt yourself it'll be your fault," Mrs. Wilson told Johnny.
7. "We'll never settle down in a big town," the Thompsons say.
8. "I think it's a good opportunity to meet new people," Ms. Harris said.
9. "How many kids do you have?" our neighbors asked us.
10. "We're going to run out of gas if we don't find a service station soon," Ann told her mother.

Total Score _____

What to say. . .

LESSON 9

CONVERSATION

STEVE: Is anybody home?

PEGGY: Up here!

STEVE: Hello, darling!

PEGGY: Whew! I'm glad that's finished. Hi! Give me a kiss. I spent the whole day straightening
5 your things. I don't know why you keep so much trash in your closet.

STEVE: Look who's talking! You'll be able to start a museum soon! But I don't want to argue. I
had a hard day and I'm looking forward to a nice hot bath . . . Hey! Where's my pink
shirt?

PEGGY: I threw it away.

10 STEVE: You threw it away?!

PEGGY: Well, one of the sleeves was a bit torn and the pocket was gone. In fact, it was so worn
out I could see right through it.*

STEVE: It was my favorite shirt! You bought it for me when . . .

PEGGY: When we got married. And that was nearly ten years ago.

15 STEVE: By the way, what have you done with my boots?

PEGGY: Well, you know Joe, the old tramp who's always looking for used things? I gave them
to him.

STEVE: But they were still in good condition.

PEGGY: Maybe. But they looked so filthy even he didn't want to take them. I had to clean them
20 first. Why don't you take your bath now and then we'll have something to eat? I'm
roasting a duck.

STEVE: Terrific! That's just what I feel like eating.

● ● ●

STEVE: Ah! I feel much better. Now where's that duck?

PEGGY: I gave it to Rufus.

25 STEVE: To the dog? But why?

PEGGY: Because it was burned. That's why! I was so busy
arguing with you that I forgot all about it.

STEVE: Never mind! We'll go to Giovanni's for dinner. What do you say?

PEGGY: That's just what I feel like doing.

---

*I could see right through it. = It was easy to see through it because the cloth was old and thin.

New Words

(to tear) (sleeve) (torn) (trash) (to roast)

(to paint) (to hide) (to put away)

(to burn) (burned) (to freeze) (frozen) (to throw away)

(neat) (messy) (down there) (up here) (up there) (down here)

DEFINITIONS

a bit: a little, not very (much)

Hey!: We use this expression when we want someone to listen to us or to stop doing something.

kiss: what two people give each other when they kiss.

Look who's talking!: so / neither are you!; so / neither + *auxiliary verb* + you!

to mess up: to make something messy or dirty.

nearly: a little less than *(He's nearly six feet tall)*; not yet but soon *(It's nearly 10:00)*.

never mind: that's all right; forget it!

to straighten (up): to make something neat or clean.

to wear out: to use something so often that it loses its color, becomes torn, etc. *(If you don't stop wearing that sweater every day, you'll wear it out)*; to make someone tired *(Running wears me out)*.

What do you say?: OK?

MINI-CONVERSATION 1

A: Have you already painted the room?
B: Yes, and I've straightened it up. Come and see for yourself.
A: I can't believe it! Where are the brushes?
B: I put them away.
A: Where did you put them?
B: In the kitchen.
A: If you don't get those brushes out of the kitchen, I'll throw them away.
B: No, you won't. They're hidden where you can't find them.

MINI-CONVERSATION 2

A: Guess what my boyfriend brought me from Paris.
B: I have no idea.
A: A gold necklace and some diamond earrings.
B: You're lucky! Show them to me.
A: I can't. They were stolen.
B: What a shame!
A: Yes, and now my boyfriend's in jail.
B: Why?
A: Well, I knew he was in Paris on business, but I didn't know what his business was!

MINI-CONVERSATION 3

A: Are you going to give them these melons?
B: Yes.
A: Why don't you give them to us instead?
B: Because I've already given you some and you threw them away.
A: Well, they were so green* we couldn't eat them.

CONVERSATION PRACTICE

About the Conversation

1. What did Peggy spend the whole day doing? Why?   2. What is Steve looking forward to? Why?   3. What did Peggy do with Steve's pink shirt? Why?   4. Was it very worn out? How do you know?   5. What did Peggy do with Steve's boots?   6. What is the tramp always looking for? Why do you think he does that?   7. Were the boots clean?   8. What is Peggy making for dinner?   9. What did Peggy do with the duck? Why?   10. What kind of food do you think they will eat at Giovanni's?

Situation 1

You are arguing with your husband / wife because he / she straightened up your things and now you don't know where anything is.

Situation 2

Your boss can't find something. He / She says you have it. You say you don't and ask him / her to look in his / her own office. He / She finds it and apologizes to you.

———
Here, green = not ready to eat.

Something bad happened at home (the food burned, the TV broke, etc.). Your husband / wife says it was your fault; you say it was his / hers. You argue about it.

SUMMARY OF NEW WORDS

VERBS: REGULAR

to burn / burned / burned   to roast / roasted / roasted
to mess up / messed up / messed up   to straighten (up) / straightened / straightened
to paint / painted / painted

VERBS: IRREGULAR

to freeze / froze / frozen   to tear / tore / torn
to hide / hid / hidden   to throw away / threw away / thrown away
to put away / put away / put away   to wear out / wore out / worn out

NOUNS			ADJECTIVES		ADVERBS
kiss(es)	sleeve(s)	trash	messy	neat	nearly

PHRASES AND EXPRESSIONS

a bit   Hey!   Look who's talking!   never mind   up / down here / there   What do you say?

EXERCISES

A. Use the right word or expression.

1. A: What are you doing?
   B: The garage is so dirty I'm going to have to *(mess it up / straighten it up)*.
2. A: Even a tramp wouldn't want this old suit. What should I do with it?
   B: *(Put it away. / Throw it away.)*
3. A: Your room is so messy that it looks like there was an explosion.
   B: *(Look who's talking! / What do you say?)*
4. A: What happened to my newspaper?
   B: The baby *(tore it / wore it out)*.
5. A: Where are the steaks I just bought?
   B: I *(burned / froze)* them because I wanted them to stay fresh.
6. A: Bobby is looking everywhere for his birthday present.
   B: That's why I *(hid / painted)* it.
7. A: You look a bit sleepy.
   B: *(I'm frozen. / I'm worn out.)*
8. A: What's wrong with your new jacket?
   B: The *(sleeve / trash)* is torn.
9. A: I guess I didn't understand the question.
   B: *(Hey! / Never mind.)* It wasn't important.

B. Choose the word or expression that doesn't belong and use it in a sentence.

1. dirty / filthy / messy / neat
2. a bit / a little / a lot / not much
3. to burn / to cook / to freeze / to roast
4. to describe / to hide / to show / to tell about
5. to keep / to put away / to save / to throw away
6. to clean / to mess up / to straighten up / to wash
7. to clean / to fix up / to paint / to tear

Grammar Summary

1. Two Object Pronouns

A. PERSONAL PRONOUNS: *me, you, him, her, it; us, you, them*

An indirect object pronoun comes before a direct object noun:

I $\begin{cases} \text{bought} \\ \text{gave} \end{cases}$ **Helen the ring.**   I $\begin{cases} \text{bought} \\ \text{gave} \end{cases}$ **her the ring.**

Or we can put the indirect object pronoun at the end and use *to* or *for*:

I $\begin{cases} \text{bought } \textbf{the ring for} \\ \text{gave } \textbf{the ring to} \end{cases}$ **Helen.**   I $\begin{cases} \text{bought } \textbf{the ring for} \\ \text{gave } \textbf{the ring to} \end{cases}$ **her.**

BUT when the *direct object is a pronoun,* we *must* use *to* or *for* with the indirect object pronoun:

I bought **it for her** / **Helen.**
I gave **it to her** / **Helen.**

SUMMARY: indirect object pronoun . . . direct object noun
     or: direct object noun . . . . . . *to / for* indirect object pronoun
     but: direct object pronoun . . . . *to / for* indirect object noun / pronoun

B. INDEFINITE PRONOUNS: *some, any, one*

I gave **Helen some fruit.** / I gave **her some.** I gave **some fruit to Helen.** / I gave **some to her.**
I didn't give **Helen any fruit.** / I didn't give **her any.** I didn't give **any fruit to Helen.** / I didn't give **any to her.**
I showed **Helen a ring.** / I showed **her one.** I showed **a ring to Helen.** / I showed **one to her.**

C. DEMONSTRATIVE PRONOUNS: *this, these; that, those*

I bought **Helen this ring.** / I bought **her this.** I bought **this ring for Helen.** / I bought **this for her.**

2. *Preposition + Object Pronoun*

We also use pronouns after prepositions: *I live **near her**; I work **for them**; Put this **next to that**; They didn't ask **for any**.*

3. *So + Adverb / Adjective (+ That)*

He drove **so carelessly (that)** he had three accidents in one month.
The crowd was **so big (that)** we couldn't swim.

4. *Past Participles as Adjectives*

We often use past participles as adjectives. They describe what happened to the noun:

a broken arm   (an arm that someone has broken)
a rented house (a house that someone has rented)
reduced prices (prices that a store has reduced)
frozen food   (food that someone has frozen)
used books   (books that have already belonged to someone else)

DEVELOPING YOUR SKILLS

A. Change the direct and indirect objects to pronouns.

1. Peggy gave Steve the shirt.
2. The movie star gave Mary and me her autograph.
3. The teacher sent John and Molly the message.
4. They gave the electrician the contract.
5. Can you lend Jane and Bill your car?
6. Mom fixed the carburetor for Hans.
7. The mechanic sold Ann and me the new tire.
8. Didn't you bring me the boots?

B. Answer the questions. Use pronouns.

Did you (*sing.*) give Steve the shirt?   *Yes, I gave it to him.*

1. Did Peggy give the tramp the boots?
2. Has your daughter told you (*sing.*) the problem?
3. Have you (*pl.*) given the children the magazines?
4. Can you (*sing.*) show us the battery?
5. Do I have to give Mr. Hunter the address?
6. Have they sent him the packages?
7. Will he bring her the tent?
8. Have they given Aunt Jane the vegetables?

C. Substitute pronouns for the italic words.

1. *Mike* showed *Mary* *his new stereo set.*
2. *Jane* didn't buy *Jack* *any chocolate.*
3. *Pete* burned *the trash* for *his mother.*
4. *I* bought *my son* *a ball.*
5. *Jane* forgot to give *her father* *his birthday present.*
6. *Frank* lent *Mary and me* *some money.*
7. *Fernando* told *the Kanes* about *his trip to Hong Kong.*
8. Did *you* send *Molly and Charlie* *a post card?*
9. *Yoko* brought *her friends* *a beautiful present.*
10. Did *you* pay *Mr. Bond* for *his work?*

D. Make sentences using the correct adverb or adjective.

the band / to play / bad / people / to go home
The band played so badly (that) the people went home.

1. Mr. Jones / to speak / soft / we couldn't hear him
2. the children / to hide / good / parents couldn't find them
3. the test / to be / hard / students couldn't answer the questions
4. the little girl / to smile / sweet / father said yes
5. the sleeve / to be / torn / I had to throw it away
6. the work / to be / urgent / they had to work all night
7. the house / to burn / quick / the firefighters couldn't stop the fire
8. Mary / to be / happy / gave me a kiss
9. Ivan / to cheer / loud / neighbors complained
10. the closet / to be / full / I couldn't put my clothes away

E. Ask and answer. Use Cue Book Chart 6. Start with *you* (sing.) / *return* / **10** / *car* / *to the manager.*

STUDENT A: Did you return the rented car to the manager?
STUDENT B: Yes, I returned it to him.

1. they / bring / **11** / man / to his children
2. carpenter / show you / **12** / closets
3. your brother / give Mary / **1** / record
4. Mrs. Lopez / show Marie / her / **2** / jeans
5. Mike / promise the other thieves / some / **3** / jewels
6. Mr. Smith / show / reporters / **4** / house
7. Dad / put / **5** / peas / fridge
8. Mr. Brown / buy / his daughter / **6** / bike
9. you (*sing.*) / mail / **7** / letters / for me
10. Peggy / give / tramp / **8** / clothes
11. you (*pl.*) / tell / them / about / **9** / gold

Talk About Yourself

1. Have you ever eaten burned food? When? What happened?   2. Do you usually wait to buy things until stores have reduced their prices? Why?   3. Do you ever buy used things? What have you bought that was used? Was it still in good condition? Was it inexpensive?   4. Are you a neat person? Do you always put your things away? Where do you put them?   5. What do you do when things get torn?   6. Do you keep a lot of old things in your closet / room / garage or do you throw them away? Why?

Test Yourself

Complete the sentences. Use *two* object pronouns in every sentence. (2 points each)

1. Concepcion couldn't type the letters, so I typed . . .
2. I bought my husband a handkerchief, but I forgot to give . . .
3. We ran out of milk, so our neighbors lent . . .
4. Raul and I didn't know where to hide the diamonds, so we asked Pablo to keep . . .
5. She knows nothing about her mother's problems, so don't tell . . .

Total Score _____

What to say . . .

LESSON 10

CONVERSATION

Mrs. Morgan wants to get a divorce. She is talking to the judge about it.

JUDGE:	Now, Mrs. Morgan, can you tell me why you want to divorce your husband?
MRS. MORGAN:	For several reasons, Your Honor. We've been living together for five years now, and I've gotten to the point where I just can't stand it anymore.
JUDGE:	Go on.
5 MRS. MORGAN:	Well, it started soon after we got married. Fred lost his job, and he's been without one ever since. I mean, he's been working off and on, but he hasn't had anything steady. He's worked in a few places because I went and got him the jobs. But he always does something wrong—on purpose, I think. He's just a lazy good-for-nothing.
10 JUDGE:	And do you work, Mrs. Morgan?
MRS. MORGAN:	Oh, yes, Your Honor. I've been working since I was eighteen. But I'm afraid I'm going to lose my job soon. I've been falling asleep at work. And it's all because of Fred. He snores so loudly that the whole house shakes. And when he doesn't snore he walks in his sleep. Last Sunday night he dreamed he was in a snow-storm and he was freezing, so he went downstairs and lit a fire in the kitchen. Fortunately I smelled the smoke and was able to put it out. I've had enough, Your Honor.
JUDGE:	Anything else?
MRS. MORGAN:	Well, on weekends, when I want to rest, he brings all his friends to the house and they sit and watch soccer on TV or play cards until late at night. They make a terrible mess. I'm just fed up.
JUDGE:	But do you still love him?
MRS. MORGAN:	I don't know. Well, maybe . . . Yes, I guess so. But I can't live on love.

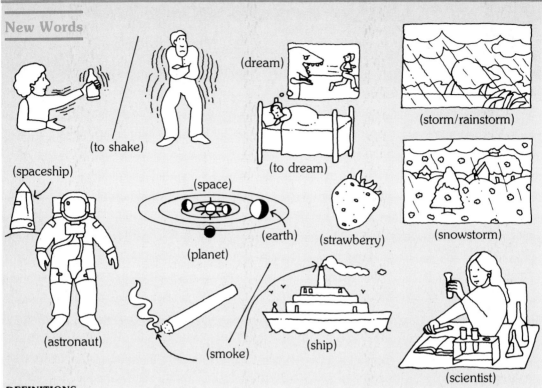

(to shake)

(spaceship)

(dream)

(to dream)

(storm/rainstorm)

(space)

(earth)

(planet)

(strawberry)

(snowstorm)

(astronaut)

(smoke)

(ship)

(scientist)

DEFINITIONS

amount: number. We use *number of* with count nouns and *amount of* with noncount nouns: *I have a large amount of money / a large number of coins.*

billion: 1,000,000,000.

can't stand: to hate.

to develop: to make something ready for the market *(They're always developing new products);* to grow, to become older or better *(A good teacher enjoys helping children develop).*

divorce: what someone gets when he or she doesn't want to be married anymore.

to divorce: to stop being married.

equipment: the things a person needs to do a job: *The only equipment you need for writing is a pen and some paper.*

ever since: *(emphatic)* since.

to fall asleep: to begin to sleep.

fed up: angry because something has happened several times.

to get a divorce (from): to divorce someone.

to get to a / the point where: We use this expression when something has been happening for so long that it can't go on anymore.

to get together: to be with someone so you can work or play together.

to go on: not to stop. We use a present participle after this expression: *They went on talking.*

good-for-nothing: a person who never works.

history: what happened in the past.

I mean: We use this expression when we are going to say something again in different words or when we are going to say why we just said something.

to launch: to put a new product on the market for the first time; to send a spaceship up.

lazy: not liking to work.

to light: to start a fire.

to lose a job: when your boss tells you that you can't work for the company anymore.

mess: where things are messy.

off and on: sometimes, but not very often.

on purpose: when a person intends to do something.

to put out a fire: to stop a fire.

reason: why you do something; why something happens.

several: more than a few; many.

sleep: when you are asleep.

to snore: to breathe noisily when you are asleep.

steady: not changing all the time.

to test: to check something to find out if it works; to give someone a test.

world: the planet Earth.

Your Honor: We say this when we are talking to a judge.

MINI-CONVERSATION 1

A: How long have the scientists been testing that equipment?

B: They've been testing it for several years now. They've tried it in fires, in storms. They've probably tested it over a thousand times.

A: Aren't they going to launch it soon? I mean, they've spent a terrific amount of time and money on it and the market's ready for it.

B: Not yet. They hope to develop a less expensive model first.

MINI-CONVERSATION 2

A: How many letters have you typed?

B: Two.

A: But you've been typing for hours!

B: Yes, but I only use two fingers.

MINI-CONVERSATION 3

A: That's a thick book you're reading. What's it about?

B: World history. I've been reading it for a week. Do you like to read?

A: Yes, but I prefer science fiction, especially about spaceships, astronauts, wars between planets . . .

B: Well, I'm happy to stay down here on earth.

CONVERSATION PRACTICE

About the Conversation

1. How long have Mr. and Mrs. Morgan been married?   2. Has Fred been working in a steady job?   3. Why does he lose his jobs so often?   4. What does Mrs. Morgan think about her husband?   5. How long has she been working?   6. Why does she think she's going to lose her

own job?   7. Why does she sleep at work?   8. What happened last Sunday?   9. Why didn't the house burn?   10. What does Fred do on the weekends?   11. Do you think Mrs. Morgan deserves a divorce? Why?

Situation 1

You are Fred Morgan. Tell the judge why you want a divorce.

Situation 2

You've been sitting in a restaurant for a long time. The waiter has already served two other people who came in after you. When he serves the third person you complain. The waiter tries to apologize, but the third person starts to argue with you.

SUMMARY OF NEW WORDS

VERBS: REGULAR

		NUMBERS
to develop / developed / developed	to launch / launched / launched	billion(s)
to divorce / divorced / divorced	to snore / snored / snored	
to dream / dreamed / dreamed	to test / tested / tested	

VERBS: IRREGULAR

to go on / went on / gone on   to light / lit / lit   to shake / shook / shaken

NOUNS

amount(s)	history	scientist(s)	space
astronaut(s)	mess(es)	ship(s)	spaceship(s)
divorce(s)	planet(s)	sleep	storm(s)
dream(s)	rainstorm(s)	smoke	strawberry (strawberries)
earth	reason(s)	snowstorm(s)	world
equipment			

PRONOUNS   ADJECTIVES

several   fed up   lazy   several   steady

PHRASES AND EXPRESSIONS

can't stand	to get to a / the point (where)	I mean	on purpose
ever since	to get together	to lose a job	to put out a fire
to fall asleep	good-for-nothing	off and on	Your Honor
to get a divorce (from)			

EXERCISES

Use the right word or expression.

1. You have to *(launch / light)* the oven if you want to cook.
2. My wife *(dreams / snores)* so noisily that I can't sleep.

3. I'm trying to find out what's in the box so I'm *(shaking / testing)* it.
4. Wherever there's *(space / smoke)* there's fire.
5. I don't have a steady job, but I've been working *(off and on / on purpose)*.
6. Let's *(get together / go on)* soon and see a movie.
7. The *(scientists / strawberries)* aren't growing because we need a good *(rainstorm / reason)*.
8. There are many billions of stars and at least nine *(planets / ships)* *(on earth / in space)*.
9. There was a large *(amount / number)* of equipment, but not a large enough *(amount / number)* of ships.
10. I drink so much coffee that I can't *(fall asleep / be fed up)*.
11. Mrs. Morgan stopped talking, but the judge told her to *(go on / get together)*.
12. They asked me why, but I didn't know the *(history / reason)*.
13. There were *(several / steady)* reasons why she wanted a divorce. The main one was that she couldn't *(develop / stand)* her husband anymore.

Grammar Summary

Present Perfect Progressive

We use this tense when something began in the past, is still happening in the present, and may go on in the future:

> I've **been waiting** for three hours. *(I began to wait three hours ago, I'm still waiting, and I'll go on waiting.)*
>
> He's **been working** since June. *(He began to work in June, he's still working, and he'll go on working.)*

We can also use the present perfect to say this *(I've **waited** for three hours. / He's **worked** since June)*. We often use the two tenses together:

> I've **been reading** for hours but I've only **read** twenty pages.
> *(I'm still reading)*   *(I'm not reading those pages anymore)*

NOTE: We don't usually use the present perfect progressive with these verbs: *to belong, to hate, to know, to like, to love, to remember, to understand.*

DEVELOPING YOUR SKILLS

A. Ask and answer. Use Cue Book Chart 1 and *for* or *since*. Start with **1** / *to steal* / *years*.

> STUDENT A: How long has he been stealing?
> STUDENT B: He's been stealing for years.

1. **2** / to cry / several minutes
2. **3** / to stand near the cashier / a short time
3. **4** / to work / 8:00
4. **5** / to look at the clothes / the store opened
5. **7** / to work here / three years
6. **8** / to talk / a minute
7. **9** / to try on make-up / a long time
8. **10** / to complain / she arrived
9. **11** / to play / they came in
10. **12** / to look at cameras / twenty minutes
11. **15** / to try to call / ten minutes
12. **16** / to lie on the floor / she fell down
13. **17** / to watch that customer / five minutes
14. **18** / to try to choose a purse / lunch

B. Ask and answer. Use Cue Book Chart 2 and *for* or *since*. Start with **18** / to fish / early this morning / / fish / to catch / only one.

> STUDENT A: How long has he been fishing?
> STUDENT B: He's been fishing since early this morning.
> STUDENT A: How many fish has he caught?
> STUDENT B: Only one.

1. **19** / to sail / hours / / miles / to sail / over twenty
2. **20** / to surf / a long time / / times / to fall / just a few
3. **1** / to sit / under the umbrella / breakfast / / times / to sit together like this / many times
4. **4** / to take / photographs / bus arrived / / to take / a lot
5. **5** / to work at the hotel / years / / suitcases / to carry / thousands
6. **7** / to stand at the bus stop / hours / / buses / to come / none
7. **8** / to walk / an hour / / cats / to see / several
8. **10** / to lie on the sand / hours / / children / to bring to the beach / two
9. **11** / to play / they got here / / holes / to make / only one
10. **14** / to sell newspapers / five minutes / / to sell / over fifty

Reading

For years countries have been developing their own spaceships. But now, for the first time in history, scientists from all over the world have gotten together. And what used to be a dream of science-fiction writers is really happening.

Three astronauts, Alexander Romanoff, from the Soviet Union, Susan King, from the United
5   States, and Lin Chen, from China, have been flying together in a spaceship for six months. The launching was a success, and they've flown over a billion miles—the greatest journey[1] in world history. They are carrying a fantastic amount of equipment and they've been testing it since they left earth. Soon they will arrive on Zenon, a planet where scientists believe they will find life.[2] The flight will go on for approximately twelve more months.

10   Although[3] the astronauts had several years of training and have learned to live and work together, they have had a few problems during the flight—not because of the computers or any of the other equipment, but because of themselves. Chen snores, and the others complain that they can't sleep. Romanoff rarely stops singing. The others can't stand it anymore because he only knows two songs. And King? Well, after several months they found out that she was going
15   to have a baby. The scientists couldn't bring them back to earth, but actually it isn't a big problem because Chen is a doctor. The trouble is that King feels like eating strawberries, and of course they don't have any. She dreams about them every night; she talks about them every day. She hopes that strawberries grow on Zenon. She has made up her mind that if they do, she will stay on that planet until her baby is born.

---

[1]Journey = trip.
[2]Life = living things.
[3]Although = even if.

About the Reading

1. What have scientists done now for the first time in history? Who used to dream about this?   2. What have the astronauts been doing for six months?   3. Have they flown far? How far?   4. What have they been doing with the equipment?   5. What do they think they may find on Zenon?   6. Have they had any trouble with the equipment?   7. What problems have they had?   8. What do you think Susan King will do? Why?   9. Do you think a journey like this can ever happen? Why?

Talk About Yourself

1. Talk about someone or something you can't stand.   2. Do you know anyone who is a good-for-nothing? Talk about him / her.   3. Why do people get divorced?   4. What do you think about flights in space? Do they help us? Are they important? Why?

Test Yourself

Make sentences with the present perfect progressive and the present perfect. Use the correct word *for* or *since*. (1 point each)

they / to sail / over a month / to stop / at ten ports
They've been sailing for over a month and they've stopped at ten ports.

1. the scientists / to test / spaceships / 1970 / (-)to launch any
2. Mary / to buy / souvenirs / an hour / to buy several
3. I / to grow / strawberries / short time / already / to sell 500 kilos
4. we / to use / this equipment / years / never / to break down
5. the children / to work / hours / only / to make / two holes
6. the astronauts / to travel / last year / already / to be / to three planets
7. I / to listen to / music / all night / only / to hear / two slow songs
8. Jack Kick / to play / soccer / ten years / (-)to score a goal
9. Tony / to train / an hour / already / to run / eight miles
10. I / to drive / I was 21 / never / to have an accident

Total Score _____

What to say . . .

Song   HELLO, HONEY

Hello, honey [E]

It's been a long long time

Since I've heard from you [A♭m]

It's been a long long time [D♭m]

5 Since I've been with you [A]

You've been living alone in my heart. [G♭] [B]

Listen, honey [E]

I've been thinking about you

All this time [A♭m]

10 You've been constantly [D♭m]

On my mind [A]

We've been so far far apart [G♭] [B]

Been so lonely [A]

Been so sad [E]

15 Have I missed you? [G♭]

Yes, I have [B]

Have I been true? [A♭m]

Yes, night and day [G♭m]

I've been wondering [A♭m]

20 What I'm going to say [A]

When I come home again. [G♭] [B]

Can you hear me? [E]

Have you thought about the things

That I wrote to you? [A♭m]

25 Have you thought about the things [D♭m]

You and I will do? [A]

Have you thought about how much [G♭]

You mean to me? [B]

LESSON 11

CONVERSATION 1

FRANK: What are you looking at?
WENDY: At that bright light in the sky.
FRANK: It looks like a plane.
WENDY: It can't be a plane, not at that speed. It must be
5   something else. I wonder what it is.
FRANK: Look! It touched the ground. It's stopped. It seems
         to be coming this way. It's coming closer!
WENDY: Do you hear that strange noise? It sounds like bees.
         Oh, Frank, I'm frightened.
10 FRANK: There's no reason to be frightened. It's probably a . . .
WENDY: Good gracious! A UFO![1] Frank! Frank, where are you?

CONVERSATION 2

WITCH A: Brain of lamb and tooth of dog . . .
WITCH B: Eye of bird and blood of frog . . .
WITCH A: Bone of man and tail of rat . . .
WITCH B: Skin of snake and fur of cat . . .
5 WITCH A: I wonder if our recipe's going to work.[2]
WITCH B: Well, it smells nice. And it looks delicious.
         Let's taste some.
WITCH A: You taste it first.
WITCH B: No, you.
10 WITCH A: Shhh! Listen! Someone's coming.
WITCH B: I can't hear anything.
WITCH A: It looks like Matilda. Yes, that's who it is. . . .
         Are you thinking what I'm thinking?
WITCH B: Yes. *(chuckling)* Hello, Matilda.
15 WITCH C: Hello, you two. You certainly look happy.
WITCH A: Yes, we're so glad to see you. How about a bowl
         of soup? You must be hungry after your journey.
WITCH C: Yes, that sounds like a good idea.
WITCH B: Here you are, dear.
20 WITCH C: Thank you. *(She begins to eat.)* Oh, it's deli- . . . !

---

[1] UFO = unidentified flying object. We pronounce this as three letters: [yuɛf'o].
[2] Here, *to work = to be a success.*

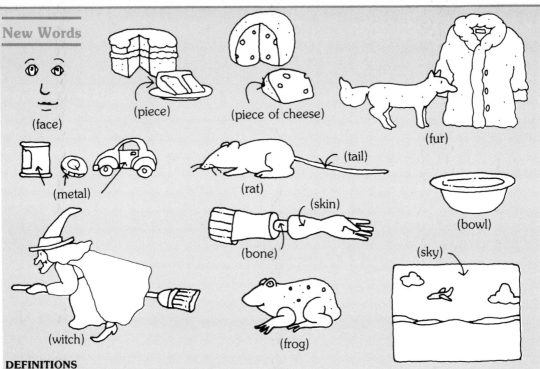

(face) (piece) (piece of cheese) (fur) (metal) (rat) (tail) (skin) (bone) (bowl) (sky) (witch) (frog)

DEFINITIONS

to appear to be: to look: *You appear to be tired. = You look tired.*

blood: if you cut yourself, you see this; it is red.

brain: what's inside your head.

bright: describes the sun, stars, lights, lamps, etc.: *The stars are bright tonight.*

to chuckle: to laugh quietly.

close (to): near.

dark: without any light; not bright.

Good gracious!: We use this expression to show great surprise.

horrible: terrible.

journey: trip.

light: what comes from the sun, from lamps, etc.; a lamp.

metal: it comes from stones, from mountains, and from the earth; gold is a metal.

to seem: to appear to be; to look: *You seem tired.*

Shhh!: Be quiet!; Don't say anything!

to sound: We use this verb to describe what we hear *(That music sounds nice)* or how something seems when we hear about it *(That sounds like a good story).*

to touch: to feel something with your hand or finger *(I touched the stove and it was hot)*; to feel something on your skin *(Something touched me)*; when two things are next to each other with no space between them *(The tree touches the house).*

UFO: something strange in the sky that may be from another planet.

way: how you do something or go somewhere: *Is this the way to the market?*

to wonder: to want to know; to ask yourself: *I wonder where Mary is.*

MINI-CONVERSATION 1

A: Bob's as busy as a bee! He studies during the day, works as a waiter at night, and still gives guitar lessons on the weekends. And how's your son?

B: Not like Bob. In fact, he seems to be getting worse. I'm afraid he's just a lazy good-for-nothing.

A: As a parent, I know how you feel.

MINI-CONVERSATION 2

A: I had a terrible dream last night. I dreamed I was inside a UFO, alone with this . . . thing. It had a frog's face and I could see through its head. The blood was moving in its brain. It had green skin, a tail, and fur on its hands. It was horrible!

B: Are you sure it was a dream? It sounds like Professor Eisenstein.

CONVERSATION PRACTICE

About Conversation 1

1. Where does Frank think the light is coming from?   2. Why can't it be a plane?   3. What does Wendy think it must be?   4. What does it sound like?   5. Why is Wendy frightened?   6. What do you think has happened to Frank?

About Conversation 2

1. Describe the witches' recipe for soup.   2. How does it smell? How does it look?   3. Why do you think the witches don't want to taste the soup?   4. Are they happy to see Matilda? Why?   5. Why do they think that Matilda must be hungry?   6. What was Matilda saying about the soup? What do you think happened to her?

Situation 1

A friend of yours has seen a UFO. (Where? / When? / What was he / she doing?) He / She tells you about the experience. You ask questions about it.

Situation 2

You have a very strange neighbor. You believe she is a witch. Tell a friend about her, what she does, and why you think she is a witch.

SUMMARY OF NEW WORDS		
VERBS: REGULAR		PREPOSITIONS
to appear / appeared / appeared	to sound / sounded / sounded	as
to chuckle / chuckled / chuckled	to touch / touched / touched	
to seem / seemed / seemed	to wonder / wondered / wondered	

NOUNS						CONJUNCTIONS
blood	brain(s)	fur(s)	metal(s)	skin(s)	UFO('s)	as
bone(s)	face(s)	journey(s)	piece(s)	sky (skies)	way(s)	
bowl(s)	frog(s)	light(s)	rat(s)	tail(s)	witch(es)	

ADJECTIVES				PHRASES AND EXPRESSIONS	
bright	close (to)	dark	horrible	Shhh!	Good gracious!

EXERCISES

A. Use Cue Book Chart 3 and any correct tense of the verb *to work*. Start with *James / 2 / for three years.*

James has been working as an electrician for three years.

1. Henry / **3** / since Mary met him
2. Ann / **may** / in that factory / **4**
3. Mr. Martin / **5** / before he got this job
4. Ralph / **6** / finishes school
5. Mr. Thompson / **7** / since 1979
6. Tony and Mike / **8** / on the weekends
7. Mrs. Smith / would like / **9**
8. My two brothers / **10** / but they don't anymore
9. Liza / **11** / for a long time
10. Peter / can't / **12** / because he doesn't know any other language besides his own
11. Yoko / **1** / for Takata Electric if the salary is good

B. Describe the pictures. Use as many new words as possible.

1.

2.

3.

4.

5.

6.

Grammar Summary

1. Can't Be / Must Be

When we think something is wrong and something else is right:

She **can't be** only eighteen. She **must be** at least twenty-five.
He **can't be** singing. He **must be** crying.

Of course we don't always use these together:

> I don't know how old she is, but she **must be** at least twenty-five.
> He was crying just a minute ago. He **can't be** singing already!

2. The Word As

You know that we use *as* to compare things (*I'm as busy as a bee; I'm not as sleepy as you are*). We can also use *as* to mean *while:*

> I remembered the key **as** I was leaving the house.
> He sang **as** he worked.

We can use *as* to mean *because:*

> **As** we had no key, we had to sleep outside.

We also use *as* as a preposition before nouns and pronouns. (NOTE: *As* describes; *like* compares.)

> I used to work **as a cook,** and all the customers ate **like horses.**

3. Verbs of Sense Perception

EYES: to look (at / like) / to watch / to see

> I was **looking at** the sky, **watching** a plane, when I **saw** something strange. It **looked** very large. It **looked like** a UFO.

EARS: to listen (to) / to hear / to sound (like)

> I was **listening to** the radio when I **heard** people shouting. It **sounded** very loud. It **sounded like** a crowd.

NOSE: to smell (like)

> I **smelled** the flowers. They **smelled** sweet. They **smelled like** honey.

MOUTH: to taste (like)

> I **tasted** the juice. It **tasted** a bit sour. It **tasted like** lemons.

FINGERS / HANDS: to touch / to feel (like)

> I **touched** the cloth. I **felt** it for a long time. It **felt** warm. It **felt like** fur.

NOTE: We can use *to seem (like)* and *to appear to be* to describe something:

> The sky **seems / appears to be** awfully dark. It **seems like / appears to be** a storm. It **seems to be / appears to be** getting worse.

We also can use *to look like* and *to sound like* to say what we think about something:

> (A shows B a marketing plan.)
> B: That **looks like** a good plan.
> (A makes a marketing suggestion.)
> B: That **sounds like** a good idea.

4. The Word *Of*

We use the word *of* in many kinds of expressions: *a picture of, a souvenir of, a tour of, tired of, on top of,* etc. We also use it in expressions of quantity: *one of, another of, some of, none of, a lot of, full of, millions of, a cup / glass / bowl / dish / plate of,* etc. We sometimes use it to show possession:

the brain **of** a lamb = a lamb**'s** brain
the office **of** the president = the president**'s** office
the captain **of** a ship = a ship**'s** captain

DEVELOPING YOUR SKILLS

A. Use Cue Book Chart 6. Start with *It doesn't look new. It / 12.*

It doesn't look new. It must be painted.

1. I can't move. I think the bone in my leg / **1**.
2. You've driven over 10,000 miles with those tires. They / **2**.
3. Those jewels can't be theirs. They / **3**.
4. We forgot the bowl in the oven. It / **4**.
5. Johnny's still playing outside. He / **5**.
6. This metal can't be new. It / **6**.
7. It feels windy in here. The tent / **8** / somewhere.
8. Those contracts / **9** / somewhere in this drawer.
9. That plane can't be theirs. It / **10**.

B. Put the following sentences together. Use *as.* After every sentence say what *as* means: *because* or *while.*

1. I turned on the light. I saw a rat eating a piece of cheese.
2. Jenny didn't like brains. She refused to eat anything.
3. He's the president of the university. He should say a few words.
4. Mrs. Tanaka spoke neither French nor English. She had to use her hands so I could understand.
5. The hijacker pulled out his gun. The pilot jumped on him.
6. The bees were close to his face. Mr. Lee just sat quietly.
7. The sky was very dark. We decided not to go for a walk.
8. We left the park. The noise of the animals seemed less loud.
9. The witches were making their medicine. They were singing softly.
10. We didn't know the way. We waited for the guide.
11. I'm an old customer. I think you should serve me first.

C. Use the cues to make sentences. Use the correct verb of sense perception.

I hear something. (train) *It sounds like a train.*
I hear something too. (awfully loud) *It sounds awfully loud.*

1. Look at that man's face. (rat)
2. I smell something. (cheese)

3. Did you taste this new recipe? (great)
4. I touched the oven. (cool)
5. Have you felt that cloth? (skin)
6. Do you hear that noise? (very close)
7. Did you see Wendy's new fur coat? (her old one)
8. Have you tasted the pudding? (terribly dry)
9. Do you smell that? (strawberries)
10. Listen to those children! (mine)
11. Do you remember the storm? (dream—use *seem*)
12. I don't know those people. (friendly—use *seem*)
13. Look at that thing in the sky over there. (spaceship—use *appear to be*)

Reading

Mr. Jones is talking about his experience with UFO's.

"It was right after a storm, and it was very dark. I went out for[1] some fresh air. As I opened the door I suddenly saw this bright light. 'It must be a broken cable,'[2] I said to myself, as there were some electric cables that went across our farm. I decided to go out and have a look. But
5 when I got to the cables, they seemed to be all right. The light was coming from another area, where some people appeared to be working. It looked like they were welding[3] something.

"As I went closer, I saw three enormous men who looked like things (or things that looked like men!). They wore face masks[4] and were fixing a broken piece of metal on a strange engine. As they didn't see me, they went on working. I knew it was dangerous, and down deep I was
10 frightened, but I went even closer and asked if they needed any help. When they saw me they got nervous and one of them made a strange noise. It sounded like 'Grr.' A friend of mine always says 'Grr' when he wants animals not to come nearer. I guessed that they didn't want me to be there, so I left. As I was leaving, I heard a noise behind me that sounded like bees. I turned and saw this large orange box. It was taking off at a fantastic speed. It wasn't a plane like
15 we have. I don't really know what it was.

"The next day I went back and found the piece of metal. It was lying on the ground, still broken. Several scientists have examined it, but they all say they've never seen anything like it. I've still got that piece of metal. I keep it in my pocket as a kind of souvenir. I wonder what it is and where it came from. I guess maybe I'll never find out."

----
[1]Here, *for* = to get.

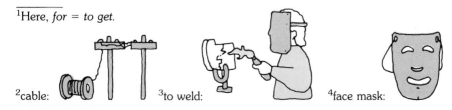

[2]cable: [3]to weld: [4]face mask:

1. Why did Mr. Jones go outside?   2. What did he see?   3. What did he think it was? Why?
4. Was there anything wrong with the cables?   5. What did the men appear to be doing?
6. What were they fixing?   7. What happened when the men saw Mr. Jones?   8. What did
Mr. Jones hear as he was leaving? What did it sound like?   9. What did he see as he turned?
10. What did he find on the ground the next day? What do scientists think about it?   11. If tomorrow you suddenly see a UFO, what will you do?

Writing

Write a conversation between yourself and someone who has just landed from another planet.

Talk About Yourself

1. Have you ever seen a UFO? Do you know anyone who has? What happened?   2. Do you
believe that there are living things on other planets? Why?   3. Do you believe that there are
witches? Do they look like the ones you've seen in pictures? What do witches do?

Test Yourself

Make sentences. (2 points each)

1. wonder / I / noise / strange / is / what / that
2. him / like / it / killing / they're / sounds
3. a / soup / they / bowl / got / of / as / they / in / came
4. we're / must / man / the / looking / he / for / be
5. never / had / bus / the / we / foot / as / on / go / came / to

Total Score _____

What to say . . .

LESSON 12

CONVERSATION

INTERVIEWER: After years and years of research, a very inexpensive means of transportation has been invented here in Utopia by Professor Jonas Kraus. Now, professor, will you give us some details of your latest invention?

PROFESSOR: Well, yes. I've designed a bicycle* that doesn't use any fuel and can be ridden in all kinds of weather.

INTERVIEWER: But all bikes can. And no bike uses any fuel.

PROFESSOR: That's where you're wrong! Ordinary bikes aren't equipped for the rain, and if you want to go uphill, you have to pedal or push. Now with my bike, you won't get wet and you won't have to push either.

INTERVIEWER: I don't understand.

PROFESSOR: You see, on my all-weather bike you're protected from the rain by a special plastic cover, and when you're tired or when you have to go up a steep hill, you just push the "save energy" button and off you go!

INTERVIEWER: That's incredible! It sounds like a wind-up toy.

PROFESSOR: Well, it is like a toy, except that you wind it up as you ride. It's made of metal, but it's very light.

INTERVIEWER: Is it already being manufactured?

PROFESSOR: Yes, it is. It's being made right here in Utopia.

INTERVIEWER: When do you expect to have it on the market?

PROFESSOR: The first model will be launched in June. For now it'll just be sold here, but later we hope to export it.

INTERVIEWER: How many models will be available?

PROFESSOR: At first, just one. But others will be produced soon. Maybe four, perhaps five other models.

INTERVIEWER: Do you use the bike yourself, professor?

PROFESSOR: Well, actually I don't. I'm afraid I've never been able to ride a bike.

*Bicycle = bike.

New Words

(air conditioner)

(button)

(made of leather)

(wood)

(uphill)

(downhill)

(made of plastic)

(made of glass)

(steep)

(hill)

(tractor)

(wool)

(cotton)

(to pedal)

(corn)

(grape)

(nylon)

(to wind (up))

(flour)

(wheat)

(exercise)

(apple)

DEFINITIONS

all-weather: ready to be used in any kind of weather.

cover: what you put over something: *When the water boils, take the cover off the pan.*

to design: to plan a dress, a building, etc.

detail: a small area of something that is larger *(You've seen the whole picture, so now let's look at the details)*; what describes something completely *(The doctor gave us all the details of the operation).*

to equip (with / for): to put the needed equipment in a factory, on a boat, etc.: *They say they equipped the plane with a computer for difficult landings.*

energy: Electricity is a kind of energy. Energy also comes from the sun, from moving water, from our bodies when they use food, etc.

except (that): but.

to export: to sell in another country.

for now: We use this expression to say that something may be different in the future.

fuel: what makes an engine work or gives energy. Gas and food are kinds of fuel.

furniture: tables, chairs, desks, bookcases, etc.

to import: to buy from companies in another country.

incredible: hard to believe, fantastic.

to invent: to design something completely new: *Marconi invented the radio.*

invention: what someone has invented.

latest: newest, most modern.

to manufacture: to make (usually in large numbers and in a factory).

means of transportation: car, bike, plane, etc.

Off you go!: you are ready to go; you can go now.

ordinary: like what you see every day, not special.

to park: to put a vehicle in a parking lot, garage, etc., turn off the engine, and leave it.

to produce: to make, to manufacture.

to protect: to keep something safe from thieves, animals, the weather, etc.

to raise: We *raise* animals; we *grow* or *raise* plants.

research: studying to learn what other people have said, done, found out, etc.

right here / there: We use this expression to make *here* and *there* clearer or stronger: *I want you to put the new equipment right here and nowhere else.*

stunning: very attractive.

vehicle: any means of transportation.

wind-up: *(adj.)* We use this to describe something that must be wound up before it will work.

MINI-CONVERSATION 1

A: What an incredible car! I've never seen one like it.
B: It's imported.
A: And just look at those seats!
B: Yes, they're not ordinary plastic. They really look like leather.
A: Is it economical?
B: I don't know. It isn't mine.

MINI-CONVERSATION 2

A: And now we have Veronica. She's wearing a white nylon blouse and a lovely green cotton skirt—both designed by Lamartine. She has a blue wool jacket and wood shoes—Lamartine's latest.
B: Aren't those shoes just stunning, dear?
C: They look dangerous to me.

MINI-CONVERSATION 3

A: This wine tastes a bit strange.
B: It's made from* apples.
A: From apples?! I thought wine was made from grapes.
B: Well, this is a special wine. I make it myself.

CONVERSATION PRACTICE

About the Conversation

1. What was invented in Utopia?   2. Who was it designed by?   3. When can the bike be ridden?   4. Why don't you get wet when you ride this bike?   5. When is the special button used?   6. What is the bike made of?   7. Where is it being produced?   8. When will it be on the market?   9. Will it be exported immediately?   10. How many models will be produced in the future?   11. Why do you think they'll wait to export it and to produce other models?
12. Does Professor Kraus enjoy riding his new invention?

Situation 1

Your house was robbed. You are reporting the robbery to the police. Tell them what was stolen or broken, if anything belonging to the thieves was left, if anybody was seen by the neighbors, etc.

Situation 2

You are selling a new invention. Tell the customer what it's made of, what it's used for, how it's used, etc. The customer will, of course, ask you questions about your new product.

SUMMARY OF NEW WORDS

VERBS: REGULAR

to design / designed / designed
to equip (for / with) / equipped / equipped
to export / exported / exported
to import / imported / imported
to invent / invented / invented
to manufacture / manufactured / manufactured

to park / parked / parked
to pedal / pedaled / pedaled
to produce / produced / produced
to protect (from) / protected / protected
to raise / raised / raised

---

*NOTE: These shoes are **made of** wood. *(It still looks like wood.)*
       This wine is **made from** apples. *(It doesn't look like apples anymore.)*

VERBS: IRREGULAR		CONJUNCTIONS		
to wind (up) / wound (up) / wound (up)		except (that)		

NOUNS

air conditioner(s)	cover(s)	fuel	invention(s)	tractor(s)
apple(s)	detail(s)	furniture	leather	vehicle(s)
button(s)	energy	glass	nylon	wheat
corn	exercise(s)	grape(s)	plastic	wood
cotton	flour	hill(s)	research	wool

ADJECTIVES   ADVERBS

all-weather	latest	steep	wind-up	downhill	uphill
incredible	ordinary	stunning			

PHRASES AND EXPRESSIONS

for now	made of	Off you go!	That's where you're wrong.
made from	means of transportation	right here / there	

EXERCISES

A. Answer.

What's this gun made of?
It's made of metal. It's a metal gun.

1. What's this suit made of?

2. What's this flour made from?

3. What's this furniture made of?

4. What's this juice made from?

5. What's this jacket made of?

6. What's this shirt made of?

7. What are these bottles made of?

8. What's this bread made from?

9. What are these shoes made of?

10. What's this wine made from?

B. Use Cue Book Chart 6. Start with *the professor / 13 / reporter*.
The professor was interviewed by the reporter.

1. the air conditioner / **1** / the electrician
2. the floor / **2** / their high heels
3. the fuel / **3** / the hijackers
4. the soldiers / **4** / the explosion
5. the grapes / **5** / the snowstorm
6. the tractors / **6** / the farmer's sons
7. the letters / **7** / our receptionist
8. the plastic cover / **8** / the storm
9. the tents / **9** / the hill
10. the vehicles / **10** / the research team
11. the politician / **11** / the police
12. this glass / **12** / my mother

Grammar Summary

1. The Passive Voice

We use the passive voice when we don't know who did something or when we want to emphasize what was done instead of who did it. The passive voice = a form of *to be* + past participle:

ACTIVE VOICE: **Someone stole** my car.   PASSIVE VOICE: My car **was stolen.**

If we want to say who did it, we can use the passive + *by: My car was stolen by someone.*

We can use the passive voice in all tenses. For example:

They keep their money in the bank. Their money **is kept** in the bank. *(simple present)*
They're keeping their money in the bank. Their money **is being kept** in the bank.
   (present progressive)
They kept their money in the bank. Their money **was kept** in the bank. *(simple past)*
They were keeping their money in the bank. Their money **was being kept** in the bank.
   (past progressive)
They'll keep their money in the bank. Their money**'ll be kept** in the bank. *(future)*

2. Impersonal You

You can't use this road. = **Nobody can use** this road. = This road **can't be used.**
You should speak English in class. = **Everybody should speak** English in class. =
   English **should be spoken** in class.

DEVELOPING YOUR SKILLS

A. Use impersonal *you* in the following sentences.

1. Those exercises can't be done.
2. That car can't be driven up a steep hill.
3. The sky can't be seen because of the pollution.
4. The furniture should be cleaned every day.
5. Plastic has to be used instead of cloth.
6. The coffee couldn't be drunk because it was so hot.
7. The UFO's had to be seen through special glasses.
8. Fruit can still be bought cheaply at the market.
9. The details couldn't be understood because they were so difficult.
10. The car shouldn't be left open at night.
11. This toy must be wound.
12. Air conditioners can be found in all the houses.

B. Say. Use Cue Book Chart 7. If more than one kind of product is shown, use the word *products*. Start with *to make* / **12** and *to manufacture* / **13**.

They make toys in Highland Park. Toys are made in Highland Park.
They manufacture fish products in Shark Bay. Fish products are manufactured in Shark Bay.

1. to test / **14**
2. to develop / **15**
3. to produce / **16**
4. to make / **17**
5. to sell / **18**

6. to manufacture / **19**
7. to sell / **20**
8. to grow / **21**
9. to make / **22**
10. to produce / **23**

11. to grow / **24**
12. to raise / **1**
13. to grow / **2**
14. to produce / **3**
15. to grow / **4**

16. to make / **5**
17. to grow / **6**
18. to raise / **7**
19. to raise / **8**
20. to manufacture / **9**

Reading

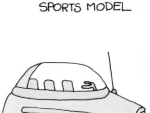

The All-Weather Bike was designed especially for you!
Safe. Comfortable. No more rain, dirt, or snow.
Your parking problems will be solved and your gas bills will be gone.
You won't have to worry about insurance either. You'll be able to get
5   your daily* exercise while going to work, to school, or to the
supermarket. And the pollution in our towns will be reduced by this
most modern and healthiest means of transportation.
A product of the latest research, the bike is equipped with a radio, an
air conditioner, special snow tires, and most important of all—the "Save
10 Energy" button. When you have to go up a steep hill or when you
want to rest, just push the button and off you go! Available in four
different models and six stunning colors. One-year warranty. For more
details, write to All-Weather Bikes, P. O. Box 1234, Utopia, Moronia.

About the Reading

1. Who was the All-Weather Bike designed for?   2. What problems will be solved if you buy an All-Weather Bike?   3. What will you be able to do while you're going to work or school?
4. What will happen because of the bike?   5. What kind of equipment does it have?   6. What is the "Save Energy" button used for?   7. When the factory gives a year's warranty, what does that mean?   8. Which model do you think will sell the most? Why?   9. Do you think the All-Weather Bike is a good idea? Why?

---

*Daily = every day.

Writing

Write to All-Weather Bikes. Tell them:

> you read about the bike *(say where / when)*
> you think it's a fantastic invention *(say why)*
> you'd like more details about it
> you'd like to know how and where you can get one

Talk About Yourself

1. Talk about your country: population, size, temperature (summer and winter), rain / snow, language(s) spoken.   2. What is produced / manufactured / grown / raised in your country? Say where. What is imported / exported? What is the largest city? Is it also the capital?   3. Now talk about your own town / city. Is it famous because of any products? Which ones? What is the largest industry? Does your country have a port? If so, what is the largest one?

Test Yourself

Make sentences. Use the passive voice and the appropriate verb. (1 point each)

to cut	to do	to give	to make	to raise
to design	to equip	to invent	to protect	to serve

wine / grapes *(present)*   *Wine is made from grapes.*

1. buildings / architects *(present)*
2. flour / wheat *(present)*
3. coffee / Brazil *(present)*
4. the electric light / Edison *(past)*
5. the prime minister / police *(past progressive)*
6. the tractor / air conditioner *(future)*
7. the corn / plastic bowl *(past)*
8. the roast beef / into small pieces *(present perfect)*
9. the details / scientists *(future)*
10. the exercises / students *(present progressive)*

Total Score _____

What to say . . .

THEY SAY IT WAS DESIGNED BY AN ASTRONAUT.

LESSON 13

MONOLOGUE 1

What would I do if I had five million Q? Man! What I could
do with five million! First, I'd take a long vacation. I'd
travel around the world and stay in the best hotels. Then
I'd buy a large house with a swimming pool—just like in the
5   movies! And I'd have two cars, one for weekdays and one for
weekends. I'd invest some of my money in real estate, and
I'd probably give some away. Of course, I wouldn't have to
work anymore, but I suppose I'd be bored if I didn't. Perhaps
I'd become a businessman.

MARTIN RYAN

MONOLOGUE 2

If I were you, dear, I wouldn't fire Pablo. I'd give him
another chance. He's been working for the company for a
long time, and he's never given you trouble in the past.
I'd talk to him, if I were you, and explain what's happening.
5   You could tell him that he's putting you in a difficult
position and that if he doesn't change, he'll have to go.
I'd rather do that than get someone else. Just think of the
time you'd save if you didn't have to train a new person.

LUZ RODRIGUEZ

MONOLOGUE 3

What would I do about inflation if I were president? Well,
I'd just freeze prices and salaries. If the government
reduced taxes and encouraged people to produce more, there'd
be more products on the market and therefore more could
5   be sold to other countries. If we just exported more than
we imported, the country would be richer and there'd be
more money available for everyone.

FRANK BERTOLDI

MONOLOGUE 4

If I could make three wishes . . . ? Now let me see. Yes,
I'd wish for health first, because if I were healthy I could
enjoy my second wish: wealth. But money couldn't buy what
I'd ask for in the third wish. I'd ask for love. What more
could you wish for?

NANCY ADAMS

(chain)

DEFINITIONS

advice: suggestion.

to encourage: to help someone feel that he/she can do something or is doing the right thing.

to explain: to tell about something so people understand.

to fire: to tell someone that he/she can't have his or her job anymore: *The boss fired me yesterday, so now I have to look for a new job.*

to freeze: to arrange for something not to change. When the government freezes prices or salaries, they can't go up. (See also Lesson 9.)

to give away: to give something, but not to any special person: *I can't sell that old couch; I guess I'll have to give it away.*

to give trouble to: to be a problem for someone.

government: the people who manage a town, city, country, etc.

health: how you feel, whether you are sick or well: *Mary is sick again; she's always in poor health.*

if I were you . . . : We often use this expression to make a suggestion.

inflation: when the cost of living goes higher and higher.

to invest: to lend money or put it in the bank and in this way to earn more.

position: where you are or how you are sitting or standing (*This is a very uncomfortable position*); job, especially compared to the other jobs in a company (*He has a much better position at the bank than he used to*). NOTE: **to be in a difficult position** = to be nervous or uncomfortable because you will have to decide something and whatever you decide, someone will be angry or hurt.

rather: prefer to: *I'd rather go tomorrow.* NOTE: We use *would* (*'d*) with *rather*. We often use *than* after *rather*: *I'd rather go than stay here.*

real estate: buildings, houses, etc., and the ground around them.

to suppose: to guess.

tax: money you have to pay to the government.

therefore: so.

to wish (for): to want or to hope for something that probably won't happen.

wish: something you want to happen that probably won't.

wealth: a lot of anything, especially money; a fortune.

weekday: any day except Saturday or Sunday.

What more . . . ?: What else?

MINI-CONVERSATION 1

A: I need your advice. I don't know what to give my wife for her birthday.

B: If I were you, I'd give her a diamond ring.

A: But that's much too expensive!

B: Well, you could buy her a nice gold chain, or . . .

A: That's still too expensive. I suppose I could buy her some flowers.

B: Plastic ones? They're cheap!

MINI-CONVERSATION 2

A: You're very lucky, Mr. Collins. We have two positions available: one in government and the other with a small company.

B: I think I'd rather work for the government. Small companies are having a difficult time because of high salaries and taxes. I was fired from my last job because of that; they thought I was earning too much money.

A: Well, I guess if I were in your position I'd choose the government job too.

CONVERSATION PRACTICE

About Monologue 1

1. What would Martin do first if he had 5,000,000 Q?   2. Where would he go?   3. What would he buy?   4. How would he invest his money?   5. What wouldn't he have to do anymore?   6. Why would Martin work?   7. What would he become?

About Monologue 2

1. What advice does Mrs. Rodriguez give her husband about Pablo?   2. How long has Pablo worked for the company?   3. Has he ever given Mr. Rodriguez trouble before?   4. What could Mr. Rodriguez tell Pablo?   5. Why does Mrs. Rodriguez suggest that he keep Pablo rather than get somebody else?

About Monologue 3

1. What would Mr. Bertoldi do about the cost of living if he were president?   2. What does he think would happen if the government reduced taxes and encouraged people to produce more? 3. How could the country get richer?   4. What would happen if the country had greater wealth?

About Monologue 4

1. What would Nancy ask for if she could make three wishes? Why?   2. What would you ask for?

Situation 1

You are the president of Moronia. Talk about the cost of living in your country. Tell why there is inflation, what people could do to reduce it, and what is being done about it by the government. (You may want to use Cue Book Chart 7 to help you.)

Situation 2

You are Mr. Rodriguez. You are talking to Pablo about his position in the company. You don't want to fire him, but you'll have to if . . . Pablo explains why he hasn't been working well, why he's been making mistakes, and why he hopes you'll give him another chance.

VERBS: REGULAR

to encourage / encouraged / encouraged
to explain / explained / explained
to fire / fired / fired

to invest / invested / invested
to suppose / supposed / supposed
to wish (for / that) / wished / wished

VERBS: IRREGULAR

to freeze / froze / frozen

ADVERBS

rather (than)   therefore

NOUNS

| advice | government(s) | inflation | real estate | wealth | wish(es) |
| chain(s) | health | position(s) | tax(es) | weekday(s) | |

PHRASES AND EXPRESSIONS

to give away   if I were you . . .   What more . . . ?
to give trouble to   in a difficult position   would rather

EXERCISES

A. Ask and answer.

use this product / design a new one

> STUDENT A: Would you use this product?
> STUDENT B: No, I'd rather design a new one.

1. shout at the children / encourage them
2. save your money / invest it
3. explain the problem to him / fire him
4. do something about it right now / discuss it first
5. like to have wealth / have good health
6. spend money on vacations / spend it on real estate
7. want to work for the government / have my own company
8. help me / give you advice

B. Answer *ad lib*. Tell which one you'd prefer and explain why.

to get married / to live alone

> *I'd rather get married than live alone (because I don't like to be alone).*
> or: *I'd rather live alone than get married (because I don't know anyone I'd like to marry).*

1. to cry / to laugh
2. to have three wishes / to have a fortune
3. to work weekends / to work nights
4. to go camping / to go on a cruise
5. to fight / to run away
6. to have a gold chain / to have a diamond ring
7. to settle down / to travel
8. to be fired / to work harder than you do now

9. to have an accident / to run out of gas
10. to be poor / to be rich and have to pay high taxes

Grammar Summary

Conditional (Type 2)

If something happened (but we don't suppose it will) or if something were true (but we don't suppose it is), then something else would happen:

If she had a lot of money, **she'd give** some of it away.
or: **She'd give** some money away **if she had** a lot of it.

In conditional sentences, we use the past tense after *if*. Note that the form of the verb *to be* is *were / weren't:*

If I were you, **I'd invest** in real estate. (not *was*)
He'd probably **fire** me **if he weren't** my friend. (not *wasn't*)

We also use *were / weren't* after *to wish:* **I wish he were** in better health.

NOTE: The conditional of *can* is *could:* **If we took** the bus, **we could** get there early.

DEVELOPING YOUR SKILLS

A. Make sentences. Use Cue Book Chart 7. Start with *I / to have / **10** / to make shoes.*

If I had leather, I'd make shoes.

1. the kids / to wear / **11** / to walk faster
2. Mr. Lee / to sell / **12** / to be rich
3. the company / to make / **14** / the government / to buy them
4. the hijacker / to explode / **15** / many people / to die
5. I / to have / **16** / to kill him
6. those factories / to produce / **17** / to make a fortune
7. I / to have / **18** / I / to make a table
8. mothers / to encourage / their children / to drink / **19** / they / to be healthier

B. Use Cue Book Chart 7. Start with *they / to have / **21** / to make cloth.*

If they had cotton, they could make cloth.

1. Mr. Jones / to buy / **22** / to be in a better position
2. Moronia / to have / **23** / to make plastic
3. we / to have / some / **24** / to make salad
4. the farmers / to grow / **1** / to sell it easily
5. the country / to export / **2** / to reduce inflation
6. Mrs. Baker / to buy / **3** / to make a cake
7. we / to have / **4** / to make wine
8. they / to import / **7** / to sell meat more cheaply

C. Use *If I were you* and answer *ad lib*. What would you say to someone who:

was robbed   *If I were you, I'd call the police.*

1. has a bad cough
2. smokes too much
3. spends too much
4. wants to get rich

5. can't sleep at night
6. was fired
7. wants to be famous
8. wants to learn English

9. wants to lose weight
10. refuses to pay taxes
11. is planning a trip
12. always forgets things

Talk About Yourself

What would you do if these things happened?

1.
2.
3.
4.

5.
6.
7.
8.

Test Yourself

Change the sentences. (2 points each)

Jack has bad health because he smokes so much.
If Jack didn't smoke so much, he wouldn't have bad health.

1. The companies can't pay better salaries because they have to pay high taxes.
2. Mary won't finish college this year because she spends all of her time at the beach.
3. There's inflation in the country because people are spending so much money.
4. Mr. Rich can't spend much time with his children because he and his wife are divorced.
5. Mr. Holden doesn't have a car, so he has to go to work by bus.

Total Score _____

What to say . . .

LESSON 14

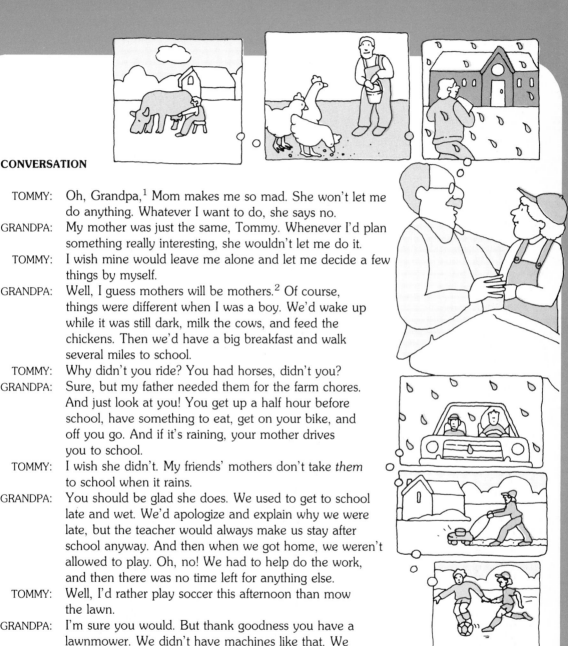

CONVERSATION

TOMMY: Oh, Grandpa,[1] Mom makes me so mad. She won't let me do anything. Whatever I want to do, she says no.

GRANDPA: My mother was just the same, Tommy. Whenever I'd plan something really interesting, she wouldn't let me do it.

5 TOMMY: I wish mine would leave me alone and let me decide a few things by myself.

GRANDPA: Well, I guess mothers will be mothers.[2] Of course, things were different when I was a boy. We'd wake up while it was still dark, milk the cows, and feed the

10 chickens. Then we'd have a big breakfast and walk several miles to school.

TOMMY: Why didn't you ride? You had horses, didn't you?

GRANDPA: Sure, but my father needed them for the farm chores. And just look at you! You get up a half hour before

15 school, have something to eat, get on your bike, and off you go. And if it's raining, your mother drives you to school.

TOMMY: I wish she didn't. My friends' mothers don't take *them* to school when it rains.

20 GRANDPA: You should be glad she does. We used to get to school late and wet. We'd apologize and explain why we were late, but the teacher would always make us stay after school anyway. And then when we got home, we weren't allowed to play. Oh, no! We had to help do the work,

25 and then there was no time left for anything else.

TOMMY: Well, I'd rather play soccer this afternoon than mow the lawn.

GRANDPA: I'm sure you would. But thank goodness you have a lawnmower. We didn't have machines like that. We

30 had to do everything by hand, and . . .

---

[1] *Grandpa* is a name we sometimes call our grandfathers; *Grandma* is for grandmothers.
[2] Grandpa is making a little joke here. We often say *boys will be boys* when a little boy does something bad.

New Words

(forward) (backward)

(to milk)

(lawnmower) (to mow (the lawn))

(king) (queen) (prince) (princess)

DEFINITIONS

to allow: to say someone can do something: *They don't allow dogs in the restaurants.* = *People can't bring their dogs into restaurants.*

anyway: even if something else happened: *I was angry, but I tried to be pleasant anyway.*

army: soldiers are in an army.

to bake: to cook in an oven: *Grandma bakes bread and cookies every week.*

by hand: without a machine.

chore: work that has to be done.

couple: two, a pair.

to dress: to put on your clothes. NOTE: **to dress up** = to put on very nice clothes.

event: something that happens (usually something important).

to feed: to give food to babies, animals, etc.

grandfather: your father's father or mother's father; Grandpa.

grandmother: your father's mother or mother's mother; Grandma.

half hour: thirty minutes.

lawn: green area near a building or house or in a park.

to leave someone alone: not to trouble someone, to let someone be by himself/herself.

left: still there after everything else is gone: *There was just one piece of bread left after the party.*

to let: to allow. NOTE: **to let someone in / on / off** = to let someone get in / on / off.

machine: cars, vacuum cleaners, refrigerators, etc. are machines.

mad: angry.

to make someone + *adj.*: to be the reason why someone is + *adj.*: *That music makes her sad / happy.*

occasion: a time when something happens.

officer: person who has a high position in the army, the police, etc.

to stay after school: when the teacher won't let you go home at the same time everyone else goes because of something you did wrong.

uniform: special clothes for your job; what soldiers, sailors, policemen, nurses, etc. wear.

willing: ready / happy to do something, not refusing, saying yes: *I'm always willing to go to the movies.*

MINI-CONVERSATION 1

A: I wish Grandmother would arrive.
B: Don't worry. She'll get here in time. She's never missed a train in her life, has she?
A: I suppose not. But I hope she remembers her passport. The last time we traveled, she lost her bus ticket and they wouldn't let her on.
B: Well, she'll probably forget something. She usually does.

MINI-CONVERSATION 2

A: Why are you all dressed up?
B: It's a special occasion—the event of the year! I was invited to Prince Rupert's wedding. Didn't you know?
A: Oh, I wish I could go with you! It would be a terrific opportunity to meet a lot of famous people.
B: I'd be willing to take you with me, but I'm afraid they wouldn't let ordinary people in.

CONVERSATION PRACTICE

About the Conversation

1. Why is Tommy complaining about his mother?   2. What does Grandpa say about *his* mother?   3. What does Tommy wish his mother would do?   4. What did Grandpa use to have to do before he went to school?   5. What does Tommy do before he goes to school?
6. What happens when it rains?   7. What would happen when Grandpa got to school late?
8. What would happen when he got home?   9. What would Tommy like to do this afternoon?
10. How did Grandpa use to mow the lawn?   11. What chores did you have to do as a child? What chores do you have to do now?

Situation

You are arguing with your grandfather / grandmother. He / She says that life was better / worse when he / she was young. You don't think so.

SUMMARY OF NEW WORDS

<u>VERBS: REGULAR</u>

to allow / allowed / allowed
to bake / baked / baked
to dress (up) / dressed (up) / dressed (up)

to milk / milked / milked
to mow / mowed / mowed

<u>VERBS: IRREGULAR</u>	<u>ADJECTIVES</u>		<u>ADVERBS</u>	
to feed / fed / fed	left	willing	anyway	forward .
to let / let / let	mad		backward	

<u>NOUNS</u>

army (armies)	grandfather(s)	half hour	machine(s)	princess(es)
chore(s)	grandma(s)	king(s)	occasion(s)	queen(s)
couple(s)	grandmother(s)	lawn(s)	officer(s)	uniform(s)
event(s)	grandpa(s)	lawnmower(s)	prince(s)	

by hand   to leave someone alone   to make someone + *adj.*   to stay after school

EXERCISES

A. Use the right word or expression.

1. I think that's the king's oldest son, *(Prince / Queen)* Jean.
2. She wanted to go, but her parents wouldn't *(feed / let)* her.
3. For parties and special occasions, Grandpa would *(mow the lawn / dress up)* in his old army *(uniform / lawnmower)*.
4. They wanted to bake a cake, but there was no flour *(allowed / left)*.
5. She was willing to go with them on two *(couples / occasions)*, but she wasn't able to.
6. Grandma didn't have any machines on her farm, so she had to milk the cows *(by hand / backward and forward)*.
7. Lawnmowers are great *(events / machines)*.
8. I wish he'd be quiet. When he talks like that he always *(leaves me alone / makes me mad)*.

B. Use the picture to tell about some of the things you would do (or would have to do) if you lived on a farm.

Grammar Summary

1. Some Uses of Would

Sometimes we use *would* instead of *used to:*

> When we were children, we **would / used to** ride to school every day.
> **I'd** always ⎫
> **I** always **used to** ⎭ forget to do my homework when I was a kid.

We sometimes stress the word *would* to show that we expected something to happen and that we aren't very happy about it:

> You **would** go there, wouldn't you?
> They **would** spend all our tax money on bombs.

2. *The Verb* To Wish

We use *to wish* + past tense to say how we would like things to be:

I wish (that) I was / were* good-looking.
We wish (that) we could wear our new uniforms.
She wishes (that) she had a lawnmower.
Don't you wish (that) you didn't have to do chores?

We use *to wish* + *would* to say how we would like things to change:

I wish (that) he wouldn't smoke in the living room.
We wish (that) you'd listen to us.
They wish (that) it wouldn't rain so often.
Grandma wishes (that) they'd talk more quietly.

DEVELOPING YOUR SKILLS

A. Ask and answer. Use Cue Book Chart 7. Start with *they* / **24** / *to sell* / *at the market.*

> STUDENT A: What did they use to do with the fruit?
> STUDENT B: They'd sell it at the market.

1. the farmers / **1** / to export / all over the world
2. Mr. Jones / **2** / to feed / to the animals
3. the factories / **3** / to put / in packages
4. your neighbors / **4** / to use / to make wine
5. Mr. Sanchez / **5** / to drink / all
6. your mother / **6** / to bake
7. the people at the supermarket / **7** / to freeze
8. you *(pl.)* / **8** / take / to the fields
9. Mrs. Panos / **9** / to use / to make sweaters and hats
10. Mr. Lee / **10** / to use / to make wallets and purses
11. the people / **11** / to leave / outside
12. your father / **12** / to fix

B. Make sentences saying you expected these things to happen. Use Cue Book Chart 3. Start with *those* / **9** / *to complain about the price of our equipment.*

Those farmers would complain about the price of our equipment.
1. those / **10** / to sell us bad fish
2. that / **11** / to give us the wrong change
3. those / **12** / to walk on the lawn
4. that / **13** / to be willing to start a fight
5. that / **14** / to wear a dirty uniform
6. that / **1** / to give us trouble
7. those / **2** / to make a mess
8. those / **3** / to use cheap wood

Informal:* I wish (that) **I was good-looking; *formal:* I wish (that) **I were** good-looking.

9. that / **4** / to put the wrong cards into the machine
10. that / **5** / to forget to turn off the water
11. those / **6** / to make a mistake like that
12. that / **7** / to let all those thieves go free
13. that / **8** / to drive backward instead of forward

C. Use Cue Book Chart 1. In which pictures are the people saying or thinking these things?

I wish they'd put the prices on. **19**

1. I wish he'd let us play with them.
2. I wish they had the latest hits here.
3. I wish they'd make longer beds.
4. I wish *my* boyfriend were as good-looking as hers is.
5. She *would* fall down the stairs!
6. I wish I had the receipt.
7. I wish the sleeves were a bit shorter.
8. I *would* choose a room where someone's dressing.
9. I wish they'd turn down that music.
10. I wish I could find my grandma.

Reading

Listen to me, children. I wish you knew how lucky you are. Things were very different when I was young. In those days couples weren't allowed to go out alone or even sit inside the house without a chaperone.[1] There would always be a younger sister or an aunt to watch us. And whenever we had a date, it was a family event. My mother would bake her special apple cake, and sometimes she'd even roast a turkey. I'd give my younger brothers and sisters their weekly[2] bath, and my father would put on his best suit for the occasion. My mother loved it, as it was a good opportunity to dress up. And my father did too, because he would have someone willing to listen to his stories and laugh at his jokes. My brothers and sisters would look forward to it as a great event because they could go to bed late. But I used to hate it. After all, it was *my* date and not my family's.

I remember the first time someone came to see me. He was an army officer and the son of a good friend of my father's, but a stranger[3] to all of us. When my mother opened the door, he kissed her hand, gave her a box of chocolates, and said, "You look lovely, my dear." He thought it was me! You see, in those days people got married very young, so my mother wasn't even forty yet. And she was especially pretty. Of course, my mother was delighted,[4] but the

---
[1]Chaperone = a person (usually a woman) who would look after an unmarried couple.
[2]Weekly = every week.
[3]Stranger = someone you don't know.
[4]Delighted = very happy.

young officer was terribly embarrassed. After that, he met the family and we went into the living room. I remember he was very good-looking. He looked like a prince in that uniform. He smiled at me and sat down. As he did, the seat of his pants tore with a terribly loud noise. He became bright red, apologized, and walked out of the room backward. I never saw him again after that. Poor man! We laughed about it for years. Whenever a young man came to visit me, my mother would ask me if I thought she should ask him to sit down or if it would be safer to let him stand up the whole time.

20

About the Reading

1. What weren't couples allowed to do when this woman was young?   2. Why was a date a family event?   3. Did the woman enjoy her dates? Why?   4. Who was her first date? 5. What happened at the door?   6. Why did the officer make a mistake?   7. What did he look like?   8. What happened when he sat down?   9. What did he do?   10. What would you do if that happened to you? What would you do if it happened to someone who was visiting you?

Talk About Yourself

1. What wouldn't your parents let you do when you were young?   2. What do you wish people wouldn't do?   3. Can you remember your first date? Tell about it.   4. Have you ever been in an embarrassing situation? Tell about it.

Test Yourself

What would you say in the following situations? Use the verb *to wish*. (2 points each)

1. Your son / daughter always walks into the house with dirty shoes.
2. A friend of yours talks too much. You are talking about him / her to another person.
3. Someone is telling you that he / she is going on a wonderful trip around the world.
4. You are trying to sleep, but you can't because your friend is listening to the radio.
5. You are at a great party, but you aren't really enjoying yourself because your boyfriend / girlfriend isn't there.

Total Score _____

What to say . . .

    A   D
I wish I were a mighty queen

                              D
I'd make your wishes come true

I wish I were a famous poet

                    A
I'd write a poem for you

              A7
5   And if I were a movie star

        D
I'd wear my jewels and my mink

                      D
And if I could I'd find the time

          E   A
To sit by the fire and think.

    A   D
I wish I were a wise old man

                        A
10   I'd have some stories to tell

                        D
I wish I were the devil himself

                      A
I'd send some people to Hell

              A7
And if I were a rich man's dog

    D
I'd have the healthiest fleas

                      D
15   And if I could I'd bring the world

          E   A
More wealth, no war, no disease.

        E
What would you do if you had the answer?
    A
    E
What would you do if you found a way?

        E
What would you do if you had a chance
        D
20   To be a happy tramp or a millionaire?
    A
To be an astronaut and fly through the air?
        D
To be an old sailor coming home from the sea?
        E
To be my sweet love and belong just to me?

I wish I were a hummingbird

                          D
25   I'd teach my young ones to fly

I wish I were a master cook

            A
I'd bake a strawberry pie

              A7
And if I were a child again

    D   A
I'd never tell Mother a lie

                      D
30   And if I could I'd always be good

          E   A
Until the day that I die.

LESSON 15

CONVERSATION

5

10

15

20

25

30

35

INTERVIEWER: Mr. President, would you tell us what you feel has been done by your government since you've been in office and what you plan to do if you're reelected?

PRESIDENT: Certainly. As you know, a lot of problems have had to be solved. But we've been very successful in solving them. Inflation has been reduced by 10 per cent,* unemployment is down, and there have been very few strikes during the last four years.

INTERVIEWER: But our industries complain that in order to reduce inflation and unemployment, foreign investments have been encouraged, and special advantages have been given to investors.

PRESIDENT: Yes, tax advantages have been given to foreign companies for a number of years, but it had to be done. Otherwise they wouldn't invest in our country. You have to understand that this is the price we must pay for development.

INTERVIEWER: What about agriculture, Mr. President?

PRESIDENT: Well, more crops were planted last year than ever before, and three hundred miles of new roads were developed in farm areas.

INTERVIEWER: Yes, farmers say that agriculture was encouraged, but at the same time, there were still high taxes on farm products.

PRESIDENT: There had to be. That's the only way we could pay for the roads.

INTERVIEWER: What about all the money spent on defense—ships and planes and bombs—when not enough was spent on health and education?

PRESIDENT: Do you think that ships and planes aren't necessary? No, sir, I can't agree with that. And besides, ten new schools and a hospital were built just this year. And I promise you that if the people of this great country vote for me again, many more schools and hospitals will be built, and so will many more houses for the poor. The prices of oil and electricity will be frozen, and . . .

---

*We sometimes use % to show *per cent*.

New Words

(to shoot)

(voter) (to vote)

(dead)

(alive)

DEFINITIONS

advantage: a better opportunity than someone else has.

to agree (with): to say that you think the same as someone else.

agriculture: the farm industry.

to break the news: to tell someone something they probably won't want to hear.

candidate: a person who wants to be elected to a position, usually in the government.

crop: what you plant; corn and wheat are crops: *This year's crop is bigger than last year's.*

defense: being ready to protect yourself if another country starts a war or someone starts a fight.

development: something that happens slowly over a long time or that is made carefully and slowly.

education: what you learn, usually in school *(He has a good education = He's learned a lot);* schools, teachers, etc. *(Our government spends a lot on education).*

to elect: to choose by voting.

election: a time when people vote.

electricity: what makes electric machines (lamps, radios, etc.) work.

ever before: *(emphatic)* before. We usually use this to compare something (an event, etc.) with what happened in the past: *More people voted in this election than ever before.*

foreign: from another country.

to inform: to tell someone about something.

information: what someone knows about something *(She has a lot of information about the election);* what you learn about something *(I got a lot of information from her).*

in office: having a position in government: *Prince Abdul was in office until this year.*

in order to: to + *infinitive: We went to the party (in order) to have a good time.*

investment: money invested, money that makes more money.

investor: someone who invests.

necessary: needed, important.

to offer: to say that you are willing to give something or do something.

to organize: to arrange.

otherwise: if not.

per cent: We use this to compare amounts; 1% = 1 / 100 (one one-hundredth) of a whole thing; 100% = the whole thing.

to plant: to put trees, flowers, etc. in the ground so they will grow.

the poor: all the poor people.

to reelect: to elect again.

result: what you get at the end of a problem, a game, an election: *We weren't happy about the result of the election because our candidate lost.*

reward: what you get when you do something well or when you find something that someone lost: *I offered a 10 Q reward to anyone who found my wallet.*

strike: when workers stop working because they want higher salaries, better working conditions, etc.

successful: having success. NOTE: **successful in** + *present participle: I was successful in finding a job.*

underwear: underpants, undershirt, bra, etc.

unemployment: when people can't get jobs: *Unemployment was at 8% = Eight per cent of the workers in the country couldn't get jobs.*

vote: what a voter gives to the candidate he / she chooses: *John Bull got more than 7,000,000 votes.*

worth: what people should be willing to pay *(The ring was worth 5,000 Q, but it was on sale for 3,500);* good or important enough *(Is it worth dying for?).* NOTE: **worth it** = even if it's difficult or costs a lot it's not too difficult or expensive: I work hard, but it's worth it.

MINI-CONVERSATION 1

A: Has the Boss been informed of the election results?

B: No, not yet. I'm going to break the news to him now.

A: I wouldn't if I were you. He's going to blow up. He was sure his candidate was going to win. Last time he won by hundreds of votes.

B: Yes, but this time the Boss wasn't there to tell the voters how to vote.

MINI-CONVERSATION 2

A: I've been offered a job at the North Pole.

B: How exciting! What will you do there?

A: I'm going to organize the new weather station and then stay there for a year.

B: Wow! Is it worth it?

A: Oh, yes! The salary's great, and it'll be a good experience. There's just one small problem.

B: What's that?

A: I can't take my family with me.

CONVERSATION PRACTICE

About the Conversation

1. What does the interviewer ask to start the interview? 2. What has been reduced and by how much? 3. What has been encouraged in the country and why? 4. What was given to the foreign investors? 5. What was done for the farmers last year? 6. What are the farmers complaining about? 7. Why does the president say the high taxes were necessary? 8. What does the interviewer wonder about health and education? 9. What does the president say about defense? 10. What does he say will be done if he is reelected? Do you think it will be done? Why?

Situation

You are a candidate in the next election. You are talking to thousands of voters at a political meeting. Say what was / wasn't done by the present government and promise what will be done if you win. The voters will ask questions that you will have to answer.

SUMMARY OF NEW WORDS

VERBS REGULAR

to agree (with) / agreed / agreed
to elect / elected / elected
to inform / informed / informed
to offer / offered / offered

to organize / organized / organized
to plant / planted / planted
to reelect / reelected / reelected
to vote / voted / voted

VERBS: IRREGULAR

to shoot / shot / shot

ADJECTIVES

alive	dead	foreign	necessary	successful	worth

ADVERBS

ever before

NOUNS

advantage(s)	development(s)	information	the poor	underwear
agriculture	education	investment(s)	result(s)	unemployment
candidate(s)	election(s)	investor(s)	reward(s)	vote(s)
crop(s)	electricity	per cent	strike(s)	voter(s)
defense				

CONJUNCTIONS

otherwise

PHRASES AND EXPRESSIONS

to break the news   in office   in order to + *inf.*   worth it

EXERCISES

Make ten sentences *ad lib.* You don't always have to use a word or expression from each group.

The candidate	agreed to informed offered to organized planted voted to	give	electricity information a reward the results tax advantages 10 per cent	to (the)	agriculture education investors the poor voters	because of about

being reelected.
being shot.
the cost of defense.
the elections.
her education.
high unemployment.
the latest development.
new information.
a poor crop.
the strike.

Grammar Summary

1. The Passive Voice: Simple Past vs. Present Perfect

Remember that the simple past tells about a definite time or an action that is finished; the present perfect tells about an indefinite time or an action that may still be going on. Both may be used in the passive voice:

They elected a new president.　　　　　A new president **was elected**.
They've elected a new president.　　　　A new president **has been elected**.

He **was elected** last week. *(definite time)*　He **has been elected**. *(indefinite time)*
A lot of people **were arrested** (during　A lot of people **have been arrested**
　the elections). *(finished action)*　　　　(since the elections). *(action that is still
　　　　　　　　　　　　　　　　　　　　　going on)*

2. Nouns Formed from Verbs

to develop → develop**ment**　　to apply → applic**ation**　　to elect → elec**tion**
to equip → equip**ment**　　　　to inform → inform**ation**　　to invent → inven**tion**
to invest → invest**ment**　　　to invite → invit**ation**　　　to suggest → sugges**tion**

DEVELOPING YOUR SKILLS

A. Use Cue Book Chart 6. Start with *crops / **4** / the army.*
The crops have been burned by the army.

1. all investments / **5** / the president
2. that fork / **6** / someone else
3. the results / **7** / the secretary
4. the curtains / **8** / the storm
5. that information / **9** / the government
6. that big building / **10** / a foreign bank
7. two voters / **11** / the police
8. the walls / **12** / a fool
9. the prime minister / **13** / three reporters
10. several windows / **1** / the men and women on strike

B. Write the correct passive form of the verb in parentheses: simple past or present perfect.

The Statue of Liberty *(to design)* by Frederic Bartholdi and *(to give)* to the American people as a present from the people of France. Bedloe's Island in New York *(to choose)* as the place for the statue to stand. (A few years ago the name of the island *(to change)* to Liberty Island.) The statue is 305 feet high and can be seen as you come into New York by ship or plane. It *(to show)* to Americans for the first time on October 28, 1886. Since then, millions of immigrants* and travelers *(to welcome)* by the bright lamp that the statue holds in its right hand. And it *(to visit)* by thousands of tourists every year. For many years people *(to allow)*

*Immigrant = person who moves to another country.

to walk up into the statue's head, but that isn't safe anymore. Many statues *(to make)* since the Statue of Liberty *(to bring)* to the United States. But few *(to put)* in a more stunning location[1] and none *(to know)* and *(to love)* by more people.

Reading

Good evening. And here's the news, brought to you by Brand X.

Today President Julian Wise of Moronia was reelected for the third time. Wise won by fewer than five hundred votes, and some of the other candidates are saying that the elections were fixed.[2] The army has been called in[3] to stop the strikes and demonstrations[4] that have been
5   organized all over the country because of the election results. It is hoped by the government that they will be successful in stopping the strikes quickly. Otherwise, even greater trouble is expected.

Twenty people have drowned, and 35 others have been badly injured[5] in this year's worst air disaster. An Air Moronia plane carrying one hundred passengers fell into the Mediterranean Sea last night near the island of Crete. Eighty passengers were saved after some Greek fishermen
10   on a ship nearby heard their urgent calls for help. The passengers were taken to the port of Khania. Most of the injured were from Moronia. They will be flown home to their families as soon as possible.

Glitter's, the large jewelry store on Swank Street, was robbed early this morning by robbers wearing only their underwear. One salesman was shot, and a customer was pushed down the
15   stairs when she refused to give them her diamond necklace. The salesman, John Sellers of 471 Grand Street, is in serious condition at Hopewell Hospital. Jewels worth more than five million Q were stolen from the store. The robbers, two men and a woman, ran away, taking the store manager with them. He was found alive late this afternoon in the trunk of the car used by the robbers. When asked about the robbery, all he could say was, "In their underwear! At Glitter's!"
20   In order to solve this robbery, all roads, ports, and airports are being watched, and a reward of 50,000 Q has been offered for any information that could help the police.

---

[1]Location = place where something is.
[2]Here, *fixed* = *arranged.*
[3]To call in = to bring together, usually to help do something.
[4]Demonstration = when people get together to show everyone how angry they are about something.
[5]To injure = to hurt.

1. How many times has President Wise been reelected?   2. Why are candidates saying the election was fixed?   3. Why has the army been called in?   4. What happened last night near Crete?   5. Were many people killed?   6. How were the passengers saved?   7. What will happen to them now?   8. Who was shot? Why do you think he was shot?   9. Why was one of the customers pushed down the stairs?   10. What happened to the store manager?   11. How were these robbers different from most robbers?

Writing

Write a news report about a recent event in your town or country.

Talk About Yourself

1. Talk about today's / yesterday's / the latest news.   2. Have you ever seen / been in a disaster? When? Where? What happened?

Test Yourself

Choose the correct form of the verb. (1 point each)

1. Another plane *(was / has been)* hijacked last night.
2. Over 100 workers *(were / have been)* arrested since the strike began.
3. The problem of unemployment *(wasn't / hasn't been)* solved by the government until this year.
4. Mr. Johnson *(was / has been)* given a reward when he found the jewels.
5. The champion *(was / has been)* found dead in his apartment early this morning.
6. These uniforms *(were / have been)* worn by Moronian soldiers during the last war.
7. Foreign investments *(were / have been)* reduced by 20 per cent since the election.
8. This job *(was / has been)* done by hand as long as I've worked here.
9. More lives *(were / have been)* saved than ever before since they found out that information.
10. Their last record *(was / has been)* produced by Scott Monroe.

Total Score _____

What to say . . .

LESSON 16

CONVERSATION

	MR. DAWSON:	It's a beautiful house. When was it built?
	MRS. SMITH:	I'm not sure. In the fifties,* I think, but we've had a lot of things done since we moved in.
	MR. DAWSON:	It looks quite new.
5	MRS. SMITH:	Yes, we had the whole place redecorated a few years ago, new wiring and a new furnace put in . . .
	MR. SMITH:	Don't forget the roof and the plumbing, dear.
	MRS. SMITH:	Oh, yes. We had new plumbing put in and a new roof put on.
10	MR. DAWSON:	I noticed the outside of the house needs painting.
	MR. SMITH:	We had it painted just last year, but with the pollution and the weather, . . . you know how it is.
	MR. DAWSON:	It's a problem, yes. How is shopping in this area?
	MRS. SMITH:	The nearest stores are about ten miles away, but
15		a new shopping center will be open soon, and that's just up the road.
	MR. DAWSON:	That's convenient. By the way, is there a school nearby?
	MRS. SMITH:	Yes, a couple of blocks away. And the bus service
20		here is great.
	MR. SMITH:	And so are the neighbors!
	MR. DAWSON:	How much are you asking for the house?
	MRS. SMITH:	75,000 Q.
	MR. DAWSON:	That's a real bargain! Do you mind if I have a
25		look upstairs?
	MRS. SMITH:	Er . . . , of course not.

● ● ●

	MR. DAWSON:	What's that noise?
	MR. SMITH:	That's just Gregory.
	MR. DAWSON:	Gregory?
30	MR. SMITH:	Yes, the previous owner.
	MR. DAWSON:	Oh, does he live with you?
	MRS. SMITH:	No, no. He's been dead for a number of years, but he loves this house, and he still comes back to see it now and then.

*The fifties = 1950–1959.

New Words

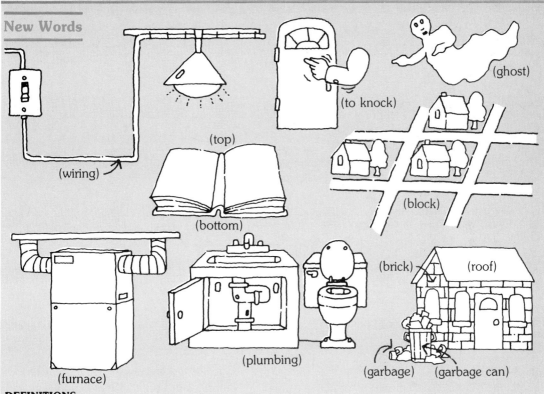

(wiring)

(top)

(bottom)

(to knock)

(ghost)

(block)

(furnace)

(plumbing)

(brick) (roof)

(garbage) (garbage can)

DEFINITIONS

away (from): from a place *(He went away)*; how far something is *(The library is two miles /
five minutes away from the museum).*

bargain: something sold at a cheap price or for less than it's really worth.

block: the four streets in a square area; one of the four streets *(If you walk down the block,
you'll see the store).*

to build: to put things together in order to make something: *He's going to use those bricks to
build a garage.*

can('t) afford: be able (not able) to buy something or do something because you (don't)
have enough money or time.

to collect: to bring together *(My sister collects stamps);* to pick up and take away *(They collect
the garbage on Tuesday).*

to disappear: not to be seen anymore; to go away: *The sky became dark when the sun disappeared.*

er . . . : a noise we make when we don't know what to say.

for sale: ready to be sold. NOTE: **on sale** = at a reduced price.

the inside: the part of something that is inside: *Let's look at the inside of the house.*

(just) up / down the road: nearby.

to manage: to be able to. (See also Lesson 7.)

to move in / out: to move into / out of an apartment, house, office, building, etc.

to notice: to see for the first time.

now and then: sometimes, but not very often.
a number of: several.
the outside: the part of something that is outside: *The outside of the window is terribly dirty.*
to own: when something belongs to you, you own it.
    owner: the person who owns something.
    previous: earlier, the one before.
    quite: very
    real: true, without any questions about it *(He's a real friend);* what really is or happens *(I don't think ghosts are real.)*
to realize: to know, to understand.
to redecorate: to paint, buy new furniture, etc. in order to fix up a house or apartment.
to service: to check and fix a machine, a car, etc.
to shop: to go to stores to buy things.
    shopping center: an area where there are many stores together so that you can do all your shopping in one place.
    store: a place where you buy things. NOTE: **department store** = a store with many departments.

MINI-CONVERSATION 1

A: Is this house still for sale?
B: No, I'm afraid it's already been sold.
A: How much was it sold for?
B: A million Q.
A: Wow! I didn't realize it was so expensive. I could never afford that.

MINI-CONVERSATION 2

A: I see Mr. Bond has disappeared. Did you manage to have the job done?
B: Yes, I did.
A: Good! What did he say about the price?
B: Nothing. But I noticed that he wasn't smiling when he went away.

CONVERSATION PRACTICE

About the Conversation

1. When was the house built?   2. What did the Smiths have done to the house?   3. What did Mr. Dawson notice?   4. How is the shopping in the area?   5. How far is the nearest school?
6. What are the neighbors like?   7. What does Mr. Dawson think of the price of the house?
8. Who is Gregory?   9. Why do you think the Smiths want to sell the house?   10. Would you buy it? Why?

Situation 1

A real estate agent is showing you a house. You talk to him / her about the house, the area, the neighbors, the price, etc.

Situation 2

A friend had his / her apartment / house redecorated. You talk about what was done and what you think of it.

SUMMARY OF NEW WORDS

VERBS: REGULAR

to collect / collected / collected
to disappear / disappeared / disappeared
to knock (on) / knocked / knocked
to manage / managed / managed
to notice / noticed / noticed

to own / owned / owned
to realize / realized / realized
to redecorate / redecorated / redecorated
to service / serviced / serviced
to shop / shopped / shopped

VERBS: IRREGULAR

to build / built / built

ADJECTIVES

previous   real

ADVERBS

away (from)   quite

NOUNS

bargain(s)	garbage	the outside	shopping center(s)
block(s)	garbage can(s)	owner(s)	store(s)
bottom(s)	ghost(s)	plumbing	top(s)
brick(s)	the inside	roof(s)	wiring
furnace(s)			

PHRASES AND EXPRESSIONS

can('t) afford   for sale   to move in / out   a number of
er . . .   (just) up / down the road   now and then

EXERCISES

A. Use the pictures to answer.

The car won't start.
You should have the battery checked.

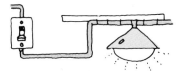

1. There's no electricity.

2. There's water on the floor.

3. The toilet doesn't work.

4. It's always cold in here.

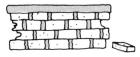

5. That wall looks weak.

B. Use the right word or expression.

1. What a terrible smell! Someone should take the *(bottom / garbage)* out.
2. I wouldn't buy that house. They say it has *(ghosts / owners)*.

3. A hundred Q is a real bargain. I know I *(can afford / can't afford)* that.
4. The *(previous / real)* owner never told me about the plumbing.
5. From the *(bottom / top)* of the mountain, you can see miles away. Why don't you *(have a look / disappear)*?
6. The house was for sale so I *(redecorated / knocked on)* the door, but no one answered.
7. My father used to *(collect / service)* coins.

C. In each group one word or phrase does not belong. Use that word or phrase in a sentence.

1. to belong to   to have   to own   to shop
2. to be able   can   can't afford   to manage
3. to fix up   to paint   to redecorate   to service
4. to go away   to leave   to move out   to settle down
5. to know   to notice   to realize   to understand
6. to appear to be   to disappear   to look like   to seem
7. to break the news   to inform   to knock   to tell
8. to build   to make   to manufacture   to realize
9. bargain   cheap   for sale   on sale
10. block   city   town   village
11. brick   garbage   metal   wood
12. plumbing   sink   toilet   wiring
13. a block away   far away   nearby   just up the road
14. away   awfully   quite   very
15. a couple of   a number of   plenty of   many
16. always   every half hour   now and then   usually

Grammar Summary

1. To Have + Noun + Past Participle

When you can't do something yourself, or you don't want to, you *have it done* for you:

I always **have my hair cut** at Figaro's.
Are you **having your apartment redecorated?**
She's **having a tooth pulled.**
Why don't you **have the plumbing fixed?**
They **had a new furnace put in.**

2. To Need + Present Participle

Sometimes we use *to need* + present participle instead of the passive:

My shoes are dirty. They **need cleaning.**   *(They need to be cleaned.)*
This machine is broken. It **needs servicing.**   *(It needs to be serviced.)*
The house **needed painting,** so I had it done.   *(It needed to be painted.)*

DEVELOPING YOUR SKILLS

A. Use Cue Book Chart 8 and the correct form: *had, is having,* or *is going to have.* Start with *the owner / the wall / 8* and *Mrs. Fernandez / the cake / 9*.

> *The owner is having the wall fixed.*
> *Mrs. Fernandez had the cake baked.*

1. Mr. Peters / a tooth / **10**
2. the manager / the hotel / **11**
3. Mrs. Jones / her car / **12**
4. Sara / her clothes / **13**
5. the hotel / the roof / **14**
6. the Chens / the plumbing / **1**
7. city / a tree / **2**

8. they / the garbage / **3**
9. they / the light / **4**
10. those rich people / their lawn / **5**
11. the man in the chair / his hair / **6**
12. the man who is coming out / his head / **6**
13. the man who is going in / his hair / **6**
14. Mr. Larsen / a new suit / **7**

B. Answer.

paint the house	What needs doing?	What did the owners have done?
	The house needs painting.	*They had the house painted.*

1. redecorate the rooms
2. mow the lawn
3. fix the fence

4. collect the garbage
5. wash the windows
6. service the furnace

7. fix the plumbing
8. check the wiring

Reading

Antonio Pereira was a young architect who worked for the town planning department in Ouro Prêto, a historic[1] town in Brazil. His job was to restore[2] old buildings.

Antonio managed to save enough money to buy one of the old houses himself. It needed a lot of work, but it was an architect's dream and was just what he wanted. They didn't have plumbing or electricity when the house was built, so Antonio had them put in. He had the whole house painted and the inside redecorated, but outside it looked the same as when he bought it: old and lovely.

[1]Historic = full of history; famous.
[2]To restore = to fix; to make like new.

After four months, the house was ready, and Antonio moved in. Some very strange things soon began to happen: Doors would suddenly open and close by themselves, even when it
10 wasn't windy. Pans and dishes would disappear from the kitchen and would later be found at the bottom of a closet or at a neighbor's house. In the middle of the night, Antonio would hear someone knocking on the door, but when he'd go to answer, no one would be there. Wherever he went in the house, he felt that someone was watching him. Then one morning as he was shaving, he saw a woman behind him in the mirror. He quickly turned around, but she was
15 gone. Antonio was very frightened. The next morning, he woke up and saw the woman sitting on his bed. He thought he was still dreaming, so he closed his eyes. When he opened them again, she was smiling at him. He moved his hand to touch her and, without a word, she disappeared. "I'm seeing things,"[1] he said to himself. But as he spoke, he realized that in fact he wasn't seeing things. He wasn't crazy. This woman was a ghost.
20 That evening when he came home, he decided to write his ghost a letter. He informed her that he couldn't afford to live anywhere else, and asked if she would be willing to let him stay in her house. He said that the place was big enough for both of them, and if she agreed, they could live there together. The letter disappeared, and so did Antonio's problems. He and his ghost, Maria Aparecida, have lived happily together ever since.

About the Reading

1. Who was Antonio Pereira, where did he live, and what was his job?   2. What did the old house need?   3. What did he have put in? Why?   4. What began to happen after Antonio moved in?   5. How did he feel about this?   6. Describe what happened when he woke up and saw the woman.   7. What did he do that evening?   8. What happened to Antonio's letter?
9. What did Antonio and Maria Aparecida decide to do?   10. What would you do in the same situation?

Writing

1. Write Antonio's letter to the ghost. *or:*   2. Use the pictures to write a ghost story.

[1]To see things = to see things that aren't real.

 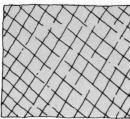  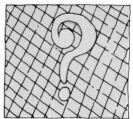

Talk About Yourself

1. What should you look for when you buy a house?   2. Would you buy a house that had ghosts?   3. Do you believe in ghosts? Are you frightened of them? Why?

Test Yourself

Complete the sentences with the correct form of one of the verbs from the list. (1 point each)

| to arrange | to equip | to fill | to move | to test |
| to build | to explain | to fire | to park | to write |

1. They had the invitation ____ by hand.
2. They'll have the tour ____ by a travel agency.
3. I had the hole ____ with sand.
4. I'm having the couch ____ into another room.
5. Here are the plans for our new house. We're having it ____ by that new young architect.
6. Of course Jose doesn't work here anymore. I had him ____.
7. Mother is having the car ____.
8. If you don't understand the problem, you should have it ____.
9. He'll have the car ____ with an air conditioner.
10. They'll have to have the machines ____ before they export them.

Total Score _____

What to say . . .

LESSON 17

CONVERSATION

SUSAN: Do you believe in fortune tellers?

RITA: Of course not! I think it's a lot of nonsense. Nobody can predict the future.

SUSAN: You're absolutely wrong. A friend of mine had his fortune
5 told by this old woman a couple of years ago, and every one of her predictions came true.

RITA: It was probably just a coincidence.

SUSAN: Well, you can find out for yourself. I'm going to see her this afternoon. Would you like to come too?

10 RITA: Sure. Why not?

● ● ●

MADAME X: I see a very bright future ahead of you, my dear, but I also see some problems.

RITA: Really? What kinds of problems?

MADAME X: You will soon lose your job, and you will have an
15 argument with your mother.

RITA: That's nothing new. We argue every day.

MADAME X: Yes, but this time you'll leave home.

RITA: What about the bright future?

MADAME X: You will get a large amount of money from a distant relative,
20 and you will meet your future husband on a journey abroad. You will have four children—I see two girls and two boys— and you will have a long and happy life.

● ● ●

RITA: Susan, this is Rita. I'm calling to let you know my new address. I've left home; I had a terrible fight
25 with my mother. I'll tell you about it sometime.

SUSAN: Yes, you must. And how's work?

RITA: Not too good. I was fired.

SUSAN: Good grief! How are you going to manage without a job and without your parents to help you?

30 RITA: Very well, actually. A cousin of my father's died and left me a fortune. I'm leaving on a cruise to the Mediterranean at the end of the month.

SUSAN: Now do you believe in fortune tellers?

RITA: Don't be silly. It's just another coincidence.

35 SUSAN: Well, have a good trip. I can't wait to meet your future husband.

New Words

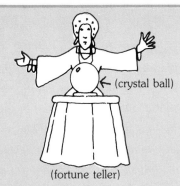

(crystal ball)

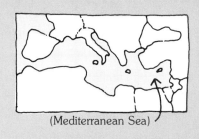

(Mediterranean Sea)

(fortune teller)

DEFINITIONS

abroad: in or to a foreign country.

absolutely: very, very much; so much that it couldn't be more.

ahead (of): coming, about to happen; in front (of), before.

argument: a fight using only words.

clear: able to be seen well, bright *(Her photos are very clear)*; able to be understood easily *(My teacher's answers are always clear)*; not cloudy *(What a clear day!)*.

coincidence: something that looks like it was planned, but wasn't.

to come true: to happen after someone has dreamed, wished, or predicted it.

cousin: your aunt and uncle's son or daughter.

distant: far, far away. *Distant relatives* are people like your grandfather's cousin. Parents, grandparents, children, aunts, uncles, brothers, sisters are *close relatives.*

every: all. We use *all* with plural nouns and *every* with singular nouns: *All the children got presents = Every child got a present* (or: *presents*).

fortune: what is going to happen to you in the future. (See also Lesson 1.)

Good grief!: Oh, no!

to leave home: to decide not to live with your family anymore.

to leave something to someone: to let someone have something after you die.

nonsense: something that doesn't mean anything or that isn't true.

positive: absolutely sure.

possibly: maybe.

to predict: to tell what will happen in the future.

prediction: something that is predicted.

relative: someone in your family (mother, father, aunt, uncle, cousin, etc.).

silly: full of nonsense.

sometime: in the future, someday. NOTE: **sometimes** = now and then, not always.

to tell someone's fortune: to predict someone's future.

That's nothing new: That always happens! That's no surprise!

MINI-CONVERSATION 1

A: Do you think Johnny will come home from school this weekend?

B: I'm sure he will. In fact, I'm absolutely positive.

A: How can you be so sure?

B: Because I didn't send him any money last week.

MINI-CONVERSATION 2

A: I see children, a big house . . .

B: How many children will I have?

A: Let me see, you'll have, . . . you'll have, . . . oh, I'm afraid my crystal ball isn't very clear.

B: Here's another 5 Q. Please try again.

A: Ah, yes, your future's suddenly very clear to me. You will marry a millionaire, you will have three healthy children, and . . . and . . .

B: Will I have a long life?

A: Possibly, but the crystal ball seems to be getting cloudy again.

CONVERSATION PRACTICE

About the Conversation

1. What does Rita think of fortune tellers? Does she believe in them?   2. What happened to Susan's friend?   3. What kind of future does Rita have ahead of her?   4. Will she have problems? What are they?   5. What else will happen?   6. Why does Rita leave home? 7. Why doesn't she need a job?   8. What is she going to do?   9. Do you think Rita believes in fortune tellers now?   10. Why does Susan think that Rita is going to get married soon?

Situation

Tell a friend's fortune. Then ask your friend to tell someone else what you said.

SUMMARY OF NEW WORDS

VERBS: REGULAR

to predict / predicted / predicted

ADVERBS

abroad   absolutely   ahead (of)   possibly

NOUNS

argument(s)	crystal ball(s)	Mediterranean (Sea)	prediction(s)
coincidence(s)	fortune	nonsense	relative(s)
cousin(s)	fortune teller(s)		

ADJECTIVES

clear   distant   every   positive   silly

PHRASES AND EXPRESSIONS

to come true	to leave something to someone	to tell someone's fortune
Good grief!	sometime	That's nothing new!
to leave home		

EXERCISES

In each group, one word or phrase does not belong. Use that word or phrase in a sentence.

1. to come true   to dream   to hope   to wish
2. to be positive   to be sure   to know   to predict
3. to go away   to leave home   to leave something to someone   to move out
4. coincidence   cousin   family   relative
5. angry discussion   argument   fight   nonsense
6. close   distant   nearby   right here
7. ahead (of)   away (from)   before   in front (of)
8. in the future   someday   sometime   sometimes
9. maybe   perhaps   possibly   probably
10. absolutely   certainly   definitely   possibly

Grammar Summary

Agreeing and Disagreeing

STATEMENT	WHEN YOU AGREE	WHEN YOU DISAGREE	WHEN YOU AREN'T SURE
I think she'll be reelected.	So do I. I do too. I'm sure she will. I'm (absolutely) positive she will. Oh, definitely. Of course (she will).	I don't. No, she won't. I don't think so. Of course she won't.	Maybe (she will). Perhaps (she will). She may. Possibly. Probably. I'm not sure. I guess / suppose so.

I don't think she'll be reelected.	Neither do I.
	 I don't either.
	 I'm sure she won't.
	 I'm (absolutely)
	     positive she won't.
	 Oh, definitely not.
	 Of course not / she
	     won't.
		I do.
		 Yes, she will.
		 Sure she will.
		 Of course she will.
			Maybe (not).
			 Maybe she won't.
			 Perhaps (not).
			 Perhaps she won't.
			 Possibly not.
			 Probably not.
			 I guess not.

DEVELOPING YOUR SKILLS

A. Agree (+), disagree (−), or say you aren't sure (?).

1. I don't think the price of gas can go any higher. (−)
2. I don't really think fortune tellers can predict the future. (+)
3. I suppose he'll become a businessman like all of his relatives. (?)
4. I don't think we'll have any arguments. (+)
5. I think the weather will be clear tomorrow. (?)
6. I don't suppose we'll travel abroad this year. (−)

7. I think your boss will realize she's wrong. (−)
8. I guess they'll have to spend an enormous amount of money. (+)
9. I don't think my cousin will ever get used to living abroad. (?)
10. I guess you'll miss us when you leave home. (−)

B. Tell what you think will happen; others will agree, disagree, or say they aren't sure. Use Cue Book Chart 5 *ad lib.*

STUDENT A: I think the plane will explode.
STUDENT B: I don't think so.

Talk About Yourself

1. Do you believe in fortune tellers? Have you ever been to one? What did he / she say?
2. Have any of your dreams or wishes ever come true? Tell about them.   3. Do many people go to fortune tellers in your country?   4. Make predictions about tomorrow's weather, about what will happen in your country, about what will happen in the world next year.

Test Yourself

What would you say? (2 points each)

1. I don't suppose they'll arrest us. *(I do too. / I guess not.)*
2. I think our new business is going to be a big success, don't you? *(Definitely. / I hope it does.)*
3. It isn't anything serious, is it, doctor? *(I suppose so. / Probably not.)*
4. I don't think she can predict what will happen. *(So do I. / Neither do I.)*
5. I forgot my umbrella. Do you think it'll rain? *(I hope so. / I hope not.)*

Total Score _____

What to say . . .

I WONDER WHAT THEY'LL BE

C   Em   A
My children will be grown someday
                              D
But I won't be there to see
G   C   F C G
The things that they will be:
C   Em   A
Good-for-nothings? Presidents?
                              D
5   But I know I won't be there
G   C
To take them by the hand
D   Am
Hoping they'll be kind
D   Am
And praying that they'll find
G   C
A castle made of stone and not of sand.

F   G
10   Will they be just what I want?
C   Am   F
Will my dreams come true?
G
If I could predict
C   C7   F
If someone knew
C
But I won't be there
C   Am
15   And when I am gone
F
Life will go on
G
Without me.

C   Em   A
My children will be grown someday
                              D
But I won't be there to hear
G   C   F C G
20   The things that they will say
C   Em   A
I wonder if they'll understand
                              D
The things I've wished for them
G   Am
When they're on their own.
D   Am
Will the dreams I've known
D   Am
25   Help them carry on
                              C
And bring love and light to their own homes?

LESSON 18

CONVERSATION 1

MRS. FIELD: I'm usually not superstitious, but I had such an awful
day yesterday that I'm really starting to believe that
Friday the thirteenth is unlucky.*

MRS. MARCH: Why? What happened?

5 MRS. FIELD: Everything went wrong. For example, I had a meeting
with an important customer this morning and on the way
to town the car broke down. When I finally got there,
the customer had already left.

MRS. MARCH: That certainly was bad luck.

10 MRS. FIELD: That's not all. This afternoon the children asked
some kids over to play and they had a pillow fight
and tore one of the pillows. When I got home there
were feathers all over.

MRS. MARCH: Good grief!

15 MRS. FIELD: Wait! There's more. Somebody—they won't say who—
had dropped a jar of jam on the new carpet. The dog
had lain down in it, so they'd given him a bath and
then put him on my bed under the electric blanket.

MRS. MARCH: Oh, no!

20 MRS. FIELD: Oh, yes! And to make matters worse, my boss and his wife
arrived while I was cleaning up the mess. I had forgotten
that I'd invited them for dinner.

CONVERSATION 2

DETECTIVE: When did you realize that something was wrong?

WATCHMAN: I noticed that the lock on Mr. Smith's office door had
been broken, so I went inside to see what had happened.

DETECTIVE: Did you touch anything?

5 WATCHMAN: Just the phone. I tried to call the police, but someone
had cut the wires!

DETECTIVE: Hadn't you heard any strange noises?

WATCHMAN: No, sir.

DETECTIVE: But they blew up the safe! I can't believe that you

10   didn't hear anything.

WATCHMAN: I guess I was asleep.

---

*Many people believe that 13 is an unlucky number, and that the thirteenth day of the month is especially
unlucky when it is on a Friday.

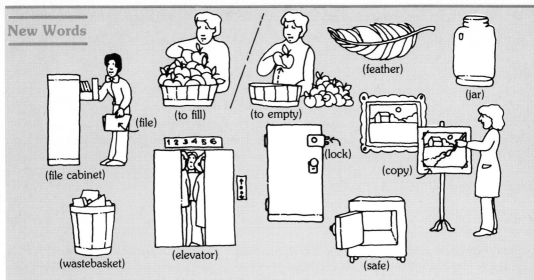

(feather)

(jar)

(file)

(to fill)

(to empty)

(file cabinet)

(lock)

(copy)

(wastebasket)

(elevator)

(safe)

DEFINITIONS

to ask someone over: to invite someone to your house.

by the time: already; before something: *I was tired by the time I got home = Before I got home I was already tired.*

carpet: rug that covers a whole floor, usually from wall to wall.

to clean up: to straighten up.

finally: last, after everything else; after waiting a long time.

for example: We say this when we are showing or explaining what we are talking about: *You should keep your money in a safe place—in a bank, for example, or in a strong safe.*

to give someone a bath: to help someone (a child, a patient) take a bath; to wash an animal.

to go right / wrong: when things happen the way we wanted them to, we say they *went right;* when they don't, they *went wrong.*

jam: a sweet food made from fruit and eaten on bread.

to make matters worse: when things are already bad and one more thing goes wrong.

night watchman: a person who stays in a building at night to protect it.

on the way: while going somewhere.

photocopier: a machine that makes copies.

so (that): in order to: *I need a key so (that) I can open the lock.*

such (a) . . . (that): that is so very (good, bad, great, terrible, etc.). The adjective that the person could have used is always clear: *They made such a mess (that) I couldn't even clean it up; It was such a surprise!*

superstitious: when you are afraid of things without a good reason or because you think they're unlucky.

unlucky: not lucky; bringing bad luck.

whether . . . or (not): if *(I didn't know whether to laugh or cry = I didn't know if I should laugh or cry);* even if *(Whether we need the machine or not, the wiring still has to be fixed = Even if we don't need the machine . . .).*

wire: long, thin piece of metal used to carry electricity.

MINI-CONVERSATION 1

A: Pete's living in Utopia now.
B: I didn't even know he'd moved.
A: Yes, he wanted to study at the university there, but I don't know whether he will or not.
B: I suppose he really moved there so that he could be with his girlfriend.

MINI-CONVERSATION 2

A: Did you manage to talk to Mr. Bond?
B: Yes. He told me to talk to Mrs. Wilson.
A: So did you see her?
B: No, she'd already left for lunch by the time I got there.
A: Why didn't you wait for her to come back?
B: Because you told me to get back here as soon as I'd spoken to Mr. Bond.

CONVERSATION PRACTICE

About Conversation 1

1. Is Mrs. Field superstitious?   2. What day was yesterday?   3. Why was she late for work?
4. What had the children done by the time she got home?   5. What had they done to the dog?
6. What was Mrs. Field doing when her boss and his wife arrived?   7. Why had they come?
8. What would you do if you had a day like that?

About Conversation 2

1. How did the night watchman know that something had happened in Mr. Smith's office?
2. What had happened to the phone?   3. How had the thieves opened the safe?   4. Why hadn't the watchman seen or heard anything?   5. Which job do you think is more interesting, the watchman's or the detective's? Which is more dangerous? Which job would you rather have? Why?

Situation 1

Your house has been robbed. Tell the police what the thieves had done by the time you got home.

Situation 2

Tell a friend about the worst experience you've ever had.

SUMMARY OF NEW WORDS

VERBS: REGULAR	CONJUNCTIONS	
to empty / emptied / emptied	so (that)	whether

ADJECTIVES			ADVERBS	
such (a / an)	superstitious	unlucky	finally	such (a / an . . . that)

EXERCISES

Use Cue Book Chart 9. Start with **4** / *to look at (−)*.

The papers hadn't been looked at.

1. **5** / to use (+)
2. **6** / to turn on (+)
3. **7** / to read (+)
4. **8** / to break (−)
5. **9** / to open (+)
6. **10** / to empty (+)
7. **11** / to turn off (−)
8. **12** / to clean (−)
9. **13** / to call (+)
10. **1** / to empty (−)
11. **2** / to cut (+)
12. **3** / to fill (+)

Grammar Summary

1. Past Perfect

We use the past perfect tense to tell about something that happened before a time in the past; it is *a past before another past.* To form the past perfect we use *had* (or: *'d*) + past participle:

PAST	EARLIER PAST
By the time I **finished** eating,	the movie **had** already **started.**
When I **got** to the office I **realized** (that)	**I'd left** my keys at home.

We also use the past perfect tense in the passive voice:

When I arrived I saw that the lock **had been broken.**

2. Such (a / an) + Noun; So + Adjective

We use *so* before an adjective and *such (a / an)* before a noun (even when there is also an adjective):

They're **such fools!** They're **so silly!**
It's **such a lovely day!** It's **so lovely** today!

We also can use a *that* clause after *so* + adjective and *such (a / an)* + noun:

They're **so silly (that)** I don't even enjoy listening to them.
It's **such a lovely day (that)** I think I'll go swimming.

3. Conjunction So (That)

We use *so (that)* to tell why:

> Speak softly **so (that)** they don't hear you.
> We're making more copies **so (that)** there will be enough.

DEVELOPING YOUR SKILLS

A. Answer.

Did you empty the ashtray? (Mary)   *Mary had already emptied it.*

1. Did you break the lock? (someone)
2. Did you clean up your room this morning? (I)
3. Did you tell that story? (John)
4. Did you make the jam? (Molly)
5. Did you pick up the feathers after the pillow fight? (my brother)
6. Did you turn off the photocopier? (the manager)
7. Did you collect the wastebaskets? (they)
8. Did you arrange for the new file cabinets? (my boss)

B. Answer. Use the passive voice.

Were you able to open the safe?   *It had already been opened by the time I got there.*

1. Did you empty the ashtray?
2. Did you fill the jars?
3. Did you cut the wires?
4. Did you collect the keys?
5. Were you able to cure the patient?
6. Did you throw away the garbage?
7. Did you fix the photocopier?
8. Did you move the file cabinets?
9. Were you able to check the plumbing?
10. Did you put away the files?
11. Did you fill the safe?
12. Did you clean up the elevators?

C. Complete the sentences with *such (a)*, *so*, *whether (. . . or not)*, or *so that*.

1. It was ____ lovely day that we wanted to stay at the beach.
2. Did she finally decide ____ she's going tomorrow?
3. They're ____ unlucky! Nothing goes right for them.
4. Finally we went downtown ____ we could buy another copy of the book.
5. ____ you hide your money under your pillow or in your closet, thieves can still find it.
6. Michael is ____ superstitious man. He won't even get out of bed on Friday the thirteenth.
7. Martha and Jim told funny stories ____ the little girl would stop crying.
8. I was ____ tired! And to make matters worse, I hadn't eaten anything.
9. ____ you clean up ____, you still can't ask anyone over this evening.
10. They were ____ incredible predictions that I didn't believe any of them.

D. Use Cue Book Chart 9 to tell what had happened in Mr. Smith's office by the time Mr. Green, the night watchman, arrived.

Talk About Yourself

1. Are you superstitious? What are you superstitious about?   2. Are you unlucky? How?
3. Do you have days when everything goes wrong? Tell about a day like that.

Test Yourself

Use Cue Book Chart 6 to make sentences in the past perfect. Start with *the children / 1 / the window by the time I / to get there.* (1 point each)

The children had broken the window by the time I got there.

1. I / **2** / my new shoes before the end of the month
2. They / **3** / the jam from the refrigerator before Mother / to get home
3. My father / **4** / holes in the carpet several times before
4. The snow / **5** / all of the food before I / to remember / that it was still outside
5. Mary / to find out / that she / **6** / all of the matches and / can(−) / light the stove
6. The secretary already / **7** / the copies before he / to leave / the office
7. She / to see / that her little brother / **8** / his clothes
8. He / to say / that he / **9** / the keys under the carpet
9. I / to know(−) / that our neighbors / **10** / a bigger house
10. They / to tell / us that they / **11** / the night watchman

Total Score _____

What to say . . .

LESSON 19

CONVERSATION

SNEAKY: Hey, Spike, what's wrong?

SPIKE: Dirty Dan got[1] my brother Sam. Somebody told on him; maybe you did, Sneaky.

SNEAKY: Not me. I wouldn't do that to Sam. You know you can
5   trust me, Spike. After all, we're friends, aren't we?

SPIKE: You're such a liar, Sneaky. I was told that Dirty Dan was here. What did he want?

SNEAKY: Nothing, Spike.

SPIKE: All right, boys.[2] Make him talk. (*Spike's men beat*
10   *Sneaky up.*)

SNEAKY: OK! OK! I did it; I told. Please make them stop, Spike. I didn't have any choice. Dirty Dan said he'd kill me.

SPIKE: What did you tell him?

15 SNEAKY: He asked me where Sam was, and I told him I hadn't seen him for months. That's all I told him. I swear, Spike!

SPIKE: Did he ask about me?

SNEAKY: He said to tell you the town was his now, and that you were finished.[3] He said that when he found you he'd
20   break *every* bone in your body.

SPIKE: Why that lousy, good-for-nothing . . . Come on, boys. We have work to do![4] (*They leave.*)

SNEAKY: (*chuckling*) It looks like I finally started a war between Spike and Dirty Dan. I don't like getting beat up, but
25   it was worth it . . . Ouch! (*Someone knocks on the door.*)

POLICE: Open up, Sneaky. This is the police. We know you're in there.

SNEAKY: What's the matter, officer?

30 POLICE: We're looking for Spike. I believe he's a friend of yours.

SNEAKY: Spike? I'm afraid I can't help you, officer. I haven't seen Spike for a long time.

POLICE: All right, men, make him talk . . .

---

[1]Here, *to get* = *to kill.*
[2]Here, *boys* = *men.*
[3]Here, *finished* = *not the boss anymore.*
[4]*Work to do* = *a job we have to do.*

DEFINITIONS

after all: isn't it true that . . . ?

to beat up: to hit someone hard and hurt him / her; to win a fight.

choice: what you choose: *My choice is the blue car.* NOTE: When you choose, you *have a choice between* things: *Our choice is between the blue car and the red one.*

to have someone do something: to tell someone that he / she should do something.

honestly: really.

How did (it) go?: How was (it)? Was everything all right?

liar: a person who tells lies.

to lie: to say something when you know it isn't true.

lie: something you say that you know isn't true.

lousy: awful, terrible.

to make someone do something: to tell someone that he / she has to do something—or else.

to open up: to open.

to swear: to promise very seriously *(I swear I'll be there on time)*; to say that you are telling the truth *(I swear that it wasn't my fault)*; to say a bad word *(Spike swore; he said "damn").*

to tell on: to tell someone that someone else has done something wrong.

to treat: to try to cure.

to trust: to believe what someone says.

truth: what is true. NOTE: **to tell the truth** = to say what is true.

MINI-CONVERSATION 1

A: How did your interview go?
B: I honestly think it went very well. They asked me if I'd ever worked in exporting and whether or not I had sales experience.
A: What did you tell them?
B: I told them I'd done both.
A: But that's a lie.
B: Well, after all, I couldn't tell them the truth, could I? I need that job.

MINI-CONVERSATION 2

A: I've done everything I could to treat the pain, Ms. Ross. I'm afraid I'm going to have to pull the tooth. It's going to hurt a little, but it'll be worth it.
B: Ouch! You said it would hurt a little. That hurt a lot.
A: I suppose you can't trust anybody nowadays. Not even your own dentist.

CONVERSATION PRACTICE

About the Conversation

1. What did Dirty Dan's boys do to Sam?   2. What does Sneaky say he wouldn't do? Would he? Did he?   3. What did Dirty Dan say he would do to Sneaky? What did he want Sneaky to tell him?   4. What did Sneaky tell him about Sam?   5. What did Dirty Dan tell Sneaky to say to Spike?   6. What do you think the job is that Spike and his boys have to do?   7. Why do you think Sneaky is happy that Spike and Dirty Dan are going to fight?   8. What do the police want to know?   9. What's going to happen to Sneaky now?

Situation 1

You had a job interview. Tell a friend about it.

Situation 2

Someone told you a terrible lie. Tell someone else about it and about why you know it's a lie.

SUMMARY OF NEW WORDS

VERBS: REGULAR   VERBS: IRREGULAR
to lie / lied / lied*   to beat (up) / beat (up) / beaten (up)
to treat / treated / treated   to trust / trusted / trusted   to swear / swore / sworn

NOUNS   ADJECTIVES   ADVERBS
choice(s)   liar(s)   lie(s)   truth   lousy   honestly

PHRASES AND EXPRESSIONS
after all   to make / have someone do something   to tell on
How did (it) go?   to open up   to tell the truth

EXERCISES

Use the right word or expression.

1. That's a lousy lie! Why don't you *(tell on me / tell the truth)*?
2. "*(Trust / Treat)* me," the dentist told the frightened little boy.
3. I worked all night, and it really wasn't *(worth it / after all)*.
4. They made me do it, Your Honor, I *(swear / tell the truth)*.
5. You have to choose between what's true and what isn't, so what's your *(truth / choice)*?
6. Spike's men *(trusted him / beat him up)* and left him on the ground.
7. Fred didn't plan to be here, but I see he came *(honestly / after all)*.
8. He didn't have a key, so he couldn't *(beat up / open up)* the box.
9. He asked me how the meeting went, but I didn't *(tell the truth / open up)*.

Grammar Summary

1. Reported Speech in the Past

DIRECT SPEECH	REPORTED SPEECH
"I **didn't lie**," he said. *(simple past)*	He said (that) he **hadn't lied**. *(past perfect)*
"I**'ve never told** a lie," she said. *(present perfect)*	She said (that) she**'d never told** a lie. *(past perfect)*
"I**'d lied** to him before," she said. *(past perfect)*	She said (that) she**'d lied** to him before. *(past perfect)*

---
*NOTE: to l**ie** → l**ying**.

2. Reported Questions in the Past

QUESTION	REPORTED QUESTION
"**Where are** your papers?" he asked me.	He asked (me) **where** my papers **were.**
"**When did you arrive?**" she asked me.	She asked (me) **when I'd arrived.**
"**Are you** a tourist?" she asked me.	She asked (me) **whether or not** / **if I was*** a tourist.
"**Do you like** the city?" he asked me.	He asked (me) **whether or not** / **if I liked** the city.

REMEMBER: In reported speech and questions, object pronouns and possessive adjectives may change:

"**Can** / **Will you show me your** ticket?" she asked me.	She asked me **whether or not** / **if I could** / **would show her my** ticket.

3. To Have / Make Someone Do Something

To have someone do something = to arrange for or to tell someone to do something.
To make someone do something = to tell someone to do something—or else!

Make him talk, boys!
The teacher **had his students read** the whole book.

DEVELOPING YOUR SKILLS

A. Report the following. Remember to change object pronouns and possessive adjectives where necessary.

1. "Where are your toys?" Mary asked the little boy.
2. "My parents never gave me a chance," Yoko told the reporter.
3. Concepcion asked Pierre, "Do you speak any other languages?"
4. "Do you want me to help you?" I asked my mother.
5. "I didn't like his swearing," the woman said.
6. "I've honestly never seen that man before," I told the police.
7. "My parents have always trusted me," she told me.
8. Then she asked us, "Are you lying?"
9. "What did you do when the fire started?" the firefighters asked them.
10. "I've been beaten up," the old man told the police.
11. "Is it worth it?" she asked.
12. "Did the others make you do it?" they asked him.
13. "Mary had already done it by the time I got there," he told me.
14. "Do you know what time it is?" I asked her.

Informal: She asked (me) **if I was** a tourist; *formal:* She asked (me) **if I were** a tourist.

B. Ask and answer. Start with *boy / to tell that lie / his brother.*

> STUDENT A: Why is the boy telling that lie?
> STUDENT B: His brother made him do it.

1. you / to lie / Dirty Dan
2. Fred / to tell the truth / the police
3. Dr. Smith / to treat the killer / the hospital
4. Maria / to tell on her friends / the teacher
5. you / to swear / this lousy job
6. he / to make that choice / somebody else
7. they / to go to that lousy movie / I

Talk About Yourself

1. Why do you think people lie? Are lies always bad?   2. Lies that we sometimes tell in order not to hurt someone are called "white lies." Have you ever told a white lie? Tell about it.
3. Do you usually trust people? Is that always a good idea?   4. Have you ever had problems because you trusted someone you shouldn't have?   5. Has anyone ever made you do something you didn't want to do? Tell about it.

Test Yourself

Report the following. (2 points each)

1. "I've never sworn in my life," she said.
2. "Are you sure?" I asked her.
3. "How long did you study at the university?" they asked me.
4. "Have you ever traveled abroad?" he asked her.
5. "I'm telling the truth," he swore.

Total Score _____

What to say . . .

Song I'D NEVER SEEN HER BEFORE

   A   E
She asked me what the time was
   A   E
And asked me what my name was
   D   A   E
She said that it was such a lovely day
   A   E
She asked me where I came from
   A   E
5 And if I had a telephone
   D   A   E
And told me that she'd like to go my way.

      A   E
And I'd never seen her before
      A   F# B7
No, I'd never seen her before.

   E
She told me she had come from very far
                   A
10 And said that she'd been traveling for a while
She'd spent a life of misery
No love, no friends, no family   (2)
   B7   E
And told me that I had a pleasant smile.

      A   E
And I'd never seen her before
      A   F# B7
15 No, I'd never seen her before.

   E
She asked me if I was a happy man
She asked me if I had a pretty wife
I told her that I lived alone
   E
And hadn't really settled down   (2)
   B7   E
20 She said she'd like to come into my life.

      A   E
And I'd never seen her before
      A   F# B7
No, I'd never seen her before.

LESSON 20

CONVERSATION

SPEAKER 1: This group has more serious problems than ever before. As you all know, the orphanage is in trouble. The money that we get from the government isn't enough to buy food and clothes for the children we have now, and there's no room for the new ones that come to live here every month. We need a new building, and we're
5   going to have to raise the money ourselves to get one. Have you any ideas?

SPEAKER 2: I think we should talk to Mr. Hope. He's an important politician, and he may be able to do something. After all, it's really the government's responsibility, and . . .

SPEAKER 1: May I say something about that?

SPEAKER 2: Of course.

10 SPEAKER 1: I'm sorry to interrupt, but I've spoken to Mr. Hope before. He promises to help, but then he doesn't do anything.

SPEAKER 3: Well, in my opinion, we should just do it ourselves. Nobody else seems to care what happens to these poor children.

SPEAKER 4: I disagree. A *lot* of people care. Last year, thirty-five children were adopted. If you
15   want my opinion, instead of building a new orphanage, we ought to try to find more good families who are willing to adopt.

SPEAKER 2: That's easier said than done.

SPEAKER 3: Why can't we go to all the hardware stores and ask them if they'll give us what we need—hammers, nails, cement? Maybe we can get wood inexpensively from a
20   lumberyard. And then, since unemployment is so high, perhaps we can find some carpenters who would be willing to do the work for very little.

SPEAKER 2: Personally, I don't think that's fair. Why should carpenters work for nothing?

SPEAKER 3: Don't worry. We wouldn't ask you. There are other carpenters in town besides you, you know.

25 SPEAKER 2: Now wait a minute! That isn't what I meant. You know I'd do anything for the orphanage. I always have. But as far as I'm concerned we can't ask people to work for nothing just because it's for a good cause.

SPEAKER 4: Listen. This group has always managed to do whatever was necessary for the children. The way I see it, if we're going to save the orphanage now, there's only
30   one thing that can help us. We ought to pray.

SPEAKER 3: Oh, for Heaven's sake!

SPEAKER 4: No, for the children's sake!

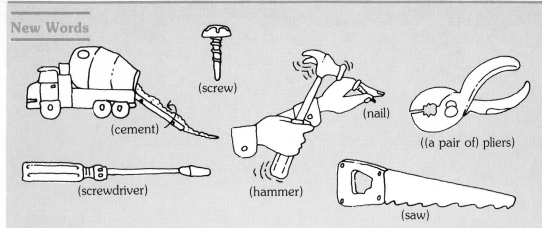

(cement) (screw) (nail) ((a pair of) pliers)

(screwdriver) (hammer) (saw)

DEFINITIONS

to adopt: to make someone else's child, or a child who has no parents, part of your family.

as far as I'm concerned: I think that . . . ; I'm only giving my opinion, but . . .

to care: to worry about, to be concerned about.

cause: something important to you; something worth working or fighting for.

concerned: worried; interested.

to disagree: not to agree.

easier said than done: We use this expression when someone suggests something that we know will be very difficult.

fair: what you deserve; the way things should be.

for a good cause: We use this expression to explain why someone should help or give money to a cause.

group: several of something that have been put together *(a group of chairs);* several people who have gotten together or who get together often to do something—for example, to discuss things, to play cards, etc.

for Heaven's sake: We use this expression when we are very surprised or fed up. NOTE: **for—'s sake** = because of someone; in order to help someone: *I'd like you to stay home for my sake; They worked hard for the children's sake.*

for nothing: without being paid for your work *(He fixed the wiring for nothing);* without having to pay *(You don't get anything for nothing nowadays).*

for very little: cheaply, for not very much money.

hardware: tools, nails, screws, etc.

to interrupt: to start talking before someone else has finished.

lumberyard: where you buy wood.

to mind your own business: not to make suggestions or give your opinion about someone else's problems. When we tell someone to do this, it is not nice.

opinion: what you think about something. NOTE: **in my (your, etc.) opinion** = what I (you, etc.) think is . . .

orphanage: a large home for many children who don't have parents.

ought to: should.

personally: as far as I'm concerned.

to raise money: to get people to give you money for something (usually a cause); to sell one thing in order to get money for something else.

responsibility: something you have to do and no one else can do: *It's his responsibility to solve that problem.*

room: area that is available for something: *You'll have to leave those files on your desk because there's no more room in the file cabinets.*

the way I see it: I think that . . .

tool: something you use in order to do something: *A vacuum cleaner is a tool for cleaning carpets.*

MINI-CONVERSATION 1

A: Sorry to trouble you, but could you possibly lend me a screwdriver and a pair of pliers?

B: Certainly. Here are the pliers, but I don't see the screwdriver anywhere.

A: Oh, never mind. I'll manage without it. Thanks.

MINI-CONVERSATION 2

A: In my opinion, Fred, I think you really ought to do something about that garage door. For your neighbors' sake, if not your own.

B: Why don't you mind your own business, Jim?

A: I'm sorry. I was only trying to help.

CONVERSATION PRACTICE

About the Conversation

MINI-CONVERSATION 3

A: The way I see it, adopting a child is an enormous responsibility.

B: No greater than having a child of your own.

A: I disagree with you. An adopted child already has problems that are someone else's fault. With your own children at least you realize where the problems came from.

B: Oh, come on! Nobody understands kids' problems—his own kids or anybody else's.

1. Why do these people need to raise money?   2. Who is Mr. Hope? Why does Speaker 2 think they ought to speak to him? What does Speaker 1 say about him?   3. What is Speaker 3's opinion? Does Speaker 4 agree?   4. What does Speaker 4 think they ought to do? How about Speaker 3?   5. Why doesn't Speaker 2 like Speaker 3's idea?   6. Why does Speaker 2 become angry?   7. What do you think of Speaker 4's idea?   8. Do you think that one of the ideas is definitely better than all the others? If so, which one?   9. How would you suggest they raise the money if you were in the group?

Situation

You have to raise money for a good cause. Ask a friend / the bank / business people to give you money. Explain what the cause is, why you need the money, and how much you need.

SUMMARY OF NEW WORDS

VERBS: REGULAR

to adopt / adopted / adopted   to disagree / disagreed / disagreed
to care / cared / cared   to interrupt / interrupted / interrupted

AUXILIARY VERBS

ought to

NOUNS

cause(s)	hardware	orphanage(s)	saw(s)
cement	lumberyard(s)	pliers	screw(s)
group(s)	nail(s)	responsibility (responsibilities)	screwdriver(s)
hammer(s)	opinion(s)	room	tool(s)

ADJECTIVES

concerned   fair

ADVERBS

personally

PHRASES AND EXPRESSIONS

as far as I'm concerned	for —'s sake	to mind your own business
easier said than done	for nothing / very little	to raise money
for a good cause	in my (your, etc.) opinion	the way I see it
for Heaven's sake		

EXERCISES

A. Tell what you need from the hardware store. Use *I ought to buy* . . .

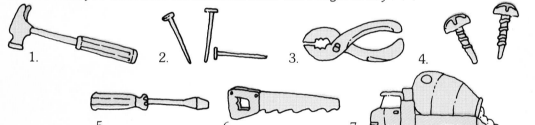

1.   2.   3.   4.

5.   6.   7.

B. Complete the sentences.

1. If you're a child without parents,
2. If you need to buy tools,
3. If you want to use nails,
4. If you have an important position,
5. If you want to use screws,
6. If you care about someone,
7. If something is not fair,
8. If you work for nothing,
9. If you say "the way I see it,"
10. If I give you advice you don't want,
11. If you see a lot of UFO's,
12. If you have an especially low salary,

a. you ought to try to change it.
b. you have a lot of responsibility.
c. you may have to live in an orphanage.
d. you go to the hardware store.
e. you'll probably give your opinion.
f. you work for very little.
g. you need a hammer.
h. you work without being paid.
i. you are concerned for him / her.
j. you may tell me to mind my own business.
k. you must have a screwdriver.
l. you may need glasses.

Auxiliary Verb: Ought To

We use *ought to,* like *should,* to show obligation and advice. We usually don't use *ought to* in questions or in negative sentences:

He **ought to study** more. = He should study more.

but: Should he study more?
He shouldn't study so much.

DEVELOPING YOUR SKILLS

A. Complete the sentences with *ought to* or *shouldn't.*

1. You ___ bring your tools. You'll need them.
2. The children ___ go to bed so late. They won't be able to get up in the morning.
3. The Browns ___ come if they don't want to.
4. Personally, I think Terry ___ stay in bed. He has a high fever.
5. You ___ drive so fast. You'll have an accident.
6. We ___ give them some money. It's for such a good cause.
7. You ___ be concerned. It's not your problem.
8. Children ___ interrupt.
9. They ___ work for nothing. They ___ ask for some money.
10. You ___ sit down. After all, there's plenty of room.

B. Use Cue Book Chart 8. Make sentences. Someone else will agree (+) or disagree (−). Start with *the city* / **4** / *to change* (±).

STUDENT A: The city ought to have the light changed.
STUDENT B: (+) Yes, they ought to.
or: (−) No, they shouldn't.

1. Mr. Rich / his **5** / to mow (+)
2. Mike / his **6** / to cut (−)
3. I / a new **7** / to make (−)
4. Mrs. Jones / her **8** / to fix (+)
5. She / the **9** / to put in a box (+)
6. you / that **10** / to pull (−)
7. we / the **11** / to paint (−)
8. I / my **12** / to service (+)
9. Mrs. Jones / her **13** / to wash (+)
10. the owners / the **14** / to fix (−)
11. they / the **1** / to fix (+)
12. we / some **2** / to plant (+)

Talk About Yourself

1. Have you ever raised money for a cause? What cause and how?   2. How much money did you need and how much did you raise?   3. Are there orphanages in your country? Do people adopt children? If not, what happens to children without parents?   4. Do you enjoy using tools? Do you like to build or fix things?   5. What kinds of things have you built? Tell about them.

What do you say? (1 point each)

1. You are listening to two friends argue about something. You disagree with both of them and want to give your opinion.
2. Someone you don't know asks how much you earn.
3. Someone is speaking and you'd like to interrupt.
4. You are at a meeting and want to tell the group what you think. How do you start?
5. Your friend talks too much and you want to tell him / her not to.
6. Someone makes a suggestion and you know it can't be done. What expression could you use?
7. A friend needs to buy some wood but doesn't know where to go. What do you suggest?
8. Someone is trying to make you decide about something, but it's really their job to decide. What could you say?
9. Your boss asks you to put something in a drawer that's already too full.
10. You belong to a group that raises money for the poor. When you ask people to give money, what do you say to make them want to give?

Total Score _____

What to say . . .

Test Yourself: Answers

1. Pleased to meet you.   2. Keep in touch!   3. I wish you the best of luck!   4. Take care!   5. By the way . . .   6. Good to see you again.   7. You look tired.   8. Likewise.   9. That's very kind of you.   10. What a shame!

LESSON 2, PAGE 13

1. funny / yourself (*or yourselves*)   2. whole / myself   3. taste / yourself (*or yourselves*)   4. for / ourselves   5. itself / service   6. worried / herself   7. sore / myself   8. themselves / put them on   9. prescription / himself   10. himself / lent

LESSON 3, PAGE 20

1. Has anything interesting happened lately?   2. I can't see. You're standing in front of me.   3. I'm very busy.   4. We're glad to have you with us.   5. Take something if you'd like it.   6. I'm excited about something.   7. Do you mind if I ask a question?   8. I hurt myself.   9. Is he good-looking?   10. What would you like to eat?

LESSON 4, PAGE 28

1. will be able   2. had to   3. was able   4. must   5. wasn't able   6. haven't had to   7. weren't able   8. didn't use to have to   9. could   10. must

LESSON 5, PAGE 36

Tell Ann to meet me at the airport, Gate 5. Ask her to bring my gun. Tell her (that) she mustn't talk to anyone. Tell her (that) I say (*or:* said) not to tell the police or my parents. Tell her (that) I say it's urgent (*or:* I said it was urgent) and (that) she must be on time. Kiku.

LESSON 6, PAGE 44

1. If the firefighters stop the fire the plane won't blow up. / If the firefighters don't stop the fire the plane will blow up. / Unless the firefighters stop the fire the plane will blow up. / Either the firefighters stop the fire or the plane will blow up.   2. If you pay attention you'll understand what I'm saying. / If you don't pay attention you won't understand what I'm saying. / Unless you pay attention you won't understand what I'm saying. / Either you pay attention or you won't understand what I'm saying.   3. If they tell him to stop he won't get hurt. / If they don't tell him to stop he'll get hurt. / Unless they tell him to stop he'll get hurt. / Either they tell him to stop or he'll get hurt.   4. If we leave quickly we'll arrive on time. / If we don't leave quickly we won't arrive on time. / Unless we leave quickly we won't arrive on time. / Either we leave quickly or we won't arrive on time.   5. If they hold their children there'll be enough seats. / If they don't hold their children there won't be enough seats. / Unless they hold their children there won't be enough seats. / Either they hold their children or there won't be enough seats.

LESSON 7, PAGE 52

1. She may not like the color.   2. She may exchange the sweater.   3. They may not listen to him.   4. He may buy an expensive camera.   5. He may not choose the latest hit.   6. He may not be able to hear.   7. She may have to go to the hospital.   8. She may not buy anything.   9. She may believe it's too expensive.   10. He may decide to try them on.

LESSON 8, PAGE 60

1. Buster says he enjoys stealing.   2. John asked me (*or:* him) if my (*or:* his) truck broke down.   3. Jerry told Mrs. Rich (that) he wouldn't be able to come (*or:* go) to the meeting.   4. Olga said (that) she was going to call Bob and me (*or:* us) as soon as they got there (*or:* here).   5. Carlos told Carol that he couldn't give her an interview until after the game.   6. Mrs. Wilson told Johnny that if he hurt himself it would be his fault.   7. The Thompsons say (that) they'll never settle down in a big town.   8. Ms. Harris said (that) she thought it was a good opportunity to meet new people.   9. Our neighbors asked us how many kids we had.   10. Ann told her mother (that) they were going to run out of gas if they didn't find a service station soon.

LESSON 9, PAGE 68

1. them for her.   2. it to him.   3. us some (*or:* some to us).   4. them for us   5. her about them

LESSON 10, PAGE 75

1. The scientists have been testing (the) spaceships since 1970 but they haven't launched any.
2. Mary has been buying souvenirs for an hour and she's bought several.   3. I've been growing strawberries for a short time and I've already sold 500 kilos.   4. We've been using this equipment for years and it's never broken down.   5. The children have been working for hours and they've only made two holes.   6. The astronauts have been traveling since last year and they've already been to three planets.
7. I've been listening to music all night and I've only heard two slow songs.   8. Jack Kick has been playing soccer for ten years and he hasn't scored a goal.
9. Tony has been training for an hour and he's already run eight miles.   10. I've been driving since I was 21 and I've never had an accident.

LESSON 11, PAGE 84

1. I wonder what that strange noise is.   2. It sounds like they're killing him.   3. They got a bowl of soup as they came in (or: As they came in they got a bowl of soup).   4. He must be the man we're looking for.   5. As the bus never came we had to go on foot.

LESSON 12, PAGE 92

1. Buildings are designed by architects.   2. Flour is made from wheat.   3. Coffee is raised in Brazil.
4. The electric light was invented by Edison.
5. The prime minister was being protected by the police.   6. The tractor will be equipped with an air conditioner.   7. The corn was served in a plastic bowl.   8. The roast beef has been cut into small pieces.   9. The details will be given by the scientists.   10. The exercises are being done by the students.

LESSON 13, PAGE 98

1. If the companies didn't have to pay high taxes, they could pay better salaries.   2. If Mary didn't spend all of her time at the beach, she'd finish college this year.   3. If people didn't spend so much money, there wouldn't be inflation in the country.
4. If Mr. Rich and his wife weren't divorced, he could spend a lot of (or: more) time with his children.   5. If Mr. Holden had a car, he wouldn't have to go to work by bus.

LESSON 14, PAGE 105

Write the sentences, then talk to your teacher.

LESSON 15, PAGE 113

1. was   2. have been   3. wasn't   4. was   5. was
6. were   7. have been   8. has been   9. have been
10. was

LESSON 16, PAGE 121

1. written   2. arranged   3. filled   4. moved
5. built   6. fired   7. parked   8. explained
9. equipped   10. tested

LESSON 17, PAGE 126

1. I guess not.   2. Definitely.   3. Probably not.
4. Neither do I.   5. I hope not.

LESSON 18, PAGE 133

1. I had worn out my new shoes before the end of the month.   2. They had stolen the jam from the refrigerator before Mother got home.   3. My father had burned holes in the carpet several times before.
4. The snow had frozen all of the food before I remembered that it was still outside.   5. Mary found out that she had used all of the matches and couldn't light the stove.   6. The secretary had already typed the copies before he left the office.
7. She saw that her little brother had torn his clothes.   8. He said that he had hidden the keys under the carpet.   9. I didn't know that our neighbors had rented a bigger house.   10. They told us that they had arrested the night watchman.

LESSON 19, PAGE 138

1. She said (that) she had never sworn in her life.
2. I asked her if she were (or: was) sure.   3. They asked me how long I'd studied at the university.
4. He asked her if she'd ever traveled abroad.
5. He swore (that) he was telling the truth.

LESSON 20, PAGE 145

Write the sentences, then talk to your teacher.

Vocabulary

The following vocabulary includes all words taught in Book III, plus all verbs taught in Books I and II. The number following each entry refers to the lesson in which that word was presented. A Roman numeral (I) or (II) following an entry means that the word was presented in Book I or II.

able: to be — (4)
aboard: Welcome —!
    (3)
abroad (17)
absolutely (17)
to adopt / —ed / —ed
    (20)
advantage(s) (15)
advice (13)
afford: can('t) — (16)
after (I;II)
    — all (19)
    hour (day, etc.) —
        hour (day,
        etc.) (8)
to agree (with) / —d /
    —d (15)
agriculture (15)
ahead (of) (17)
air conditioner(s) (12)
alive (15)
all (II)
    after — (19)
    — over adv. (1);
        adj. (6)
to allow / —ed / —ed
    (14)
all-weather (12)
alone (II)
    to leave someone
        — (14)
altitude (3)
ambulance(s) (4)
amount(s) (10)
to answer / —ed / —ed
    (II)
anyway (14)
to apologize / —d / —d
    (II)
to appear / —ed / —ed
    (11)
apple(s) (12)
to apply / —ied / —ied
    (for) (II)
approximately (3)
Arab(s) (6)
to argue / —d / —d (I)

argument(s) (17)
army (armies) (14)
to arrange (for / to) / —d /
    —d (3)
to arrest / —ed / —ed (6)
to arrive / —d / —d (I)
as conj. & prep. (11)
    — far — I'm con-
        cerned (20)
    do — I say (6)
    not half — + adj. /
        adv. + — (7)
to ask / —ed / —ed (II)
    to — for (8)
    to — someone
        over (18)
asleep (II)
    to fall — (10)
astronaut(s) (10)
at (I)
    — first (7)
    — least (8)
ate see to eat
attention: to pay —
    (6)
autograph(s) (8)
available (4)
away (16)
    — from (16)
    to give — (13)
    to put — (9)
    to run — (6)
    to throw — (9)

back adv. (4)
    — home (3)
    to go — to work
        (7)
backward (14)
to bake / —d / —d (14)
ball(s) (II)
    crystal —(s) (17)
bargain(s) (16)
bath (I)
    to give someone a
        — (18)

battery (batteries) (4)
to be / was (were) / been
    (I)
to beat (up) / beat / beat-
    en (19)
to become / became / be-
    come (II)
been see to be
before (I;II)
    ever — (15)
to begin / began / begun
    (II)
to believe / —d / —d (7)
to belong / —ed / —ed (6)
best (II)
    for the — (7)
    to wish someone
        the — of luck
        (1)
billion(s) (10)
a bit (9)
blade(s): razor — (2)
blew up see to blow
    up
block(s) (16)
blood (11)
to blow up / blew up /
    blown up (6)
to board / —ed / —ed (I)
bomb(s) (6)
bone(s) (11)
Boom! (6)
boot(s) (2)
to bore / —d / —d (II)
to borrow / —ed / —ed
    (something
    from someone)
    (II)
bottom(s) (16)
bought see to buy
bowl(s) (11)
brain(s) (11)
to break / broke / broken
    (II)
    to — down (4)
    to — the news (15)
to breathe / —d / —d (II)

brick(s) (16)
bright (11)
to bring / brought /
    brought (II)
broke(n) see to break
brought see to bring
to brush / —ed / —ed (II)
to build / built / built (16)
to burn / —ed / —ed (9)
business(es) (II)
    to mind your own
        — (20)
button(s) (12)
to buy / bought / bought
    (I)
by (I)
    — + time (6)
    — hand (14)
    — the time (18)
    — the way (1)
    embarrassed — (8)
    Who is it —? (2)

cabinet(s): file — (18)
to call / —ed / —ed (II)
    to be —ed (3)
cameraman (men) (6)
to camp / —ed / —ed (3)
camper(s) (3)
campground(s) (3)
camping: to go — (3)
can('t) / could(n't) (II)
    —('t) afford (16)
    —'t stand (10)
    —'t wait (to / for)
        (3)
can(s): garbage —
    (16)
candidate(s) (15)
captain(s) (3)
carburetor(s) (4)
to care / —d / —d (20)
    care: Take —! (1)
carpenter(s) (1)
carpet(s) (18)
to carry / —ied / —ied (II)

to cash /—ed /—ed (I)
cashier(s) (1)
to catch / caught / caught (II)
cause(s) (20)
  for a good — (20)
cement (20)
cent: per — (15)
center(s): shopping — (16)
chain(s) (13)
chance(s) (5)
  to give someone a — (5)
to change /—d /—d (II)
change(s) (3)
to check /—ed /—ed (4)
  to — in (I)
to cheer /—ed /—ed (8)
choice(s) (19)
to choose / chose / chosen (II)
chore(s) (14)
chose(n) see to choose
to chuckle /—d /—d (11)
to clean /—ed /—ed (II)
  to — up (18)
clear (17)
to close /—d /—d (II)
close (to) (11)
coach(es) (8)
coincidence(s) (17)
to collect /—ed /—ed (16)
college(s) (1)
to comb /—ed /—ed (II)
to come / came / come (I)
  — on! (2)
  to — true (17)
to compare /—d /—d (II)
to complain /—ed /—ed (II)
computer programmer(s) (1)
concerned (20)
  as far as I'm — (20)
condition(s) (8)
  in good (bad, etc.) — (8)
conditioner(s): air — (12)
contract(s) (5)
convenient (5)
to cook /—ed /—ed (I)
copy (copies) (18)

corn (12)
to cost / cost / cost (II)
cotton (12)
could (II;4)
couple(s) (14)
cousin(s) (17)
cover(s) (12)
crop(s) (15)
crowd(s) (8)
crowded (3)
to cry / cried / cried (II)
crystal ball(s) (17)
cup(s) (I;8)
to cure /—d /—d (2)
to cut / cut / cut (2)

Damn! (4)
to dance /—d /—d (I)
dark (11)
Darn! (2)
day after day (8)
dead (15)
deaf (6)
dear (3)
to decide /—d /—d (7)
to declare /—d /—d (I)
deep (7)
  — down (7)
defense (15)
definitely (7)
degree(s) (3)
it depends (4)
deposit(s) (4)
to describe /—d /—d (II)
to deserve /—d /—d (7)
to design /—ed /—ed (12)
desk(s) (5)
detail(s) (12)
to develop /—ed /—ed (10)
development(s) (15)
to dial /—ed /—ed (II)
did see to do
to die /—d /—d (II)
dirt (4)
to disagree /—d /—d (20)
to disappear /—ed /—ed (16)
to discuss /—ed /—ed (5)
distant (17)
to divorce /—d /—d (10)

divorce(s) (10)
  to get a — (from) (10)
to do / did / done (I)
  — as I say (6)
  to — with (7)
done: easier said than — (20)
down (II)
  to break — (4)
  deep — (7)
  — here / there (9)
  — the road (16)
  to fall — (2)
  to settle — (7)
downhill (12)
drank see to drink
drawer(s) (5)
to dream /—ed /—ed (10)
dream(s) (10)
to dress (up) /—ed /—ed (14)
to drink / drank / drunk (I)
to drive / drove / driven (I)
to drop /—ped /—ped (2)
drove see to drive
to drown /—ed /—ed (3)
drunk see to drink

to earn /—ed /—ed (II)
earth (10)
easier said than done (20)
to eat / ate / eaten (I)
education (15)
either . . . or (5)
to elect /—ed /—ed (15)
election(s) (15)
electrician(s) (1)
electricity (15)
elevator(s) (18)
else (I)
  or — (6)
embarrassed (by) (8)
embarrassing (8)
to empty /—ied /—ied (18)
to encourage /—d /—d (13)
energy (12)

engine(s) (4)
to enjoy /—ed /—ed (II)
to equip (for / with) / —ped /—ped (12)
equipment (10)
er . . . (16)
especially (8)
estate: real — (13)
event(s) (14)
ever (II)
  — before (15)
  — since (10)
every (17)
to examine /—d /—d (II)
example: for — (18)
excellent (2)
except prep. (II)
  — (that) conj. (12)
to exchange /—d /—d (II)
exercise(s) (12)
to expect /—ed /—ed (II)
experience (5)
to explain /—ed /—ed (13)
explosion(s) (6)
to export /—ed /—ed (12)

face(s) (11)
fact: in — (4)
fair(s) (5)
fair (20)
to fall / fell / fallen (2)
  to — asleep (10)
  to — down (2)
far (from) (3)
  as — as I'm concerned (20)
farmer(s) (1)
feather(s) (18)
fed see to feed
fed up (10)
to feed / fed / fed (14)
to feel (that) / felt / felt (II;8)
  to — like + -ing (7)
fell see to fall
felt see to feel
field(s) (8)
file(s) (18)
  — cabinet(s) (18)

to fill /—ed /—ed (4)
  — it up (4)
  to — out (II)
finally (18)
to find (that) / found /
      found (II;8)
  to — out (II)
to finish /—ed /—ed (I)
to fire /—d /—d (13)
  fire(s) (3)
    to put out a — (10)
  firefighter(s) (1)
first (I)
  at — (7)
to fish /—ed /—ed (I)
  fisherman (men) (1)
to fix /—ed /—ed (II)
  to — up (7)
flat (4)
flew see to fly
floor(s) (6)
flour (12)
to fly / flew / flown (I)
folks (3)
for (I)
  to ask — (8)
  — a good cause
    (20)
  — example (18)
  — Heaven's sake
    (20)
  — nothing / very
    little (20)
  — now (12)
  — sale (16)
  — (someone)'s
    sake (20)
  — the best / worst
    (7)
  to wish — (13)
foreign (15)
to forget / forgot / forgot-
    ten (II)
fortune(s) (1;17)
  — teller(s) (17)
  to tell someone's
    — (17)
forward (14)
  to look — to (3)
to freeze / froze / frozen
    (9;13)
friend(s) (I)
  to make —s (7)
frightened (6)
frog(s) (11)

from (I)
  away — (16)
  far — (3)
  made — (12)
froze(n) see to freeze
fuel (12)
fur(s) (11)
furnace(s) (16)
furniture (12)

garbage (16)
  — can(s) (16)
gas (4)
gave see to give
to get / got / gotten (II)
  to — a divorce
    (from) (10)
  to — hurt (6)
  to — to a / the
    point (where)
    (10)
  to — together (10)
  to — used to + -ing
    (7)
ghost(s) (16)
to give / gave / given (II)
  to — away (13)
  to — someone a
    bath (18)
  to — someone a
    chance (5)
  to — trouble to
    (13)
glass (I;12)
to go / went / gone (I)
  to — back to work
    (7)
  to — camping (3)
  to — on (10)
  to — right / wrong
    (18)
  to — sailing (3)
  How did (it) —?
    (19)
  Off you —! (12)
goal(s) (8)
good (I)
  for a — cause (20)
  — gracious! (11)
  — grief! (17)
  — luck! (8)
good-for-nothing (10)
goodness: Thank —!
    (6)

government(s) (13)
gracious: Good —!
    (11)
grandfather(s) (14)
grandma(s) (14)
grandmother(s) (14)
grandpa(s) (14)
grape(s) (12)
grew see to grow
grief: Good —! (17)
group(s) (20)
to grow / grew / grown (1)
guide: tour —(s) (1)
guy(s) (6)
  smart —(s) (6)

had see to have
half:
  — hour (14)
  not — as + adj. /
    adv. + as (7)
hammer(s) (20)
hand(s) (II)
  by — (14)
to hang up / hung up /
    hung up (II)
to happen /—ed /—ed
    (II)
hardware (20)
to hate /—d /—d (I)
to have / had / had (I)
  to — a seat (5)
  to — someone do
    something (19)
health (13)
to hear / heard / heard
    (II)
Heaven: for —'s
    sake (20)
heel(s) (2)
held see to hold
helicopter(s) (6)
to help /—ed /—ed (II)
  to — yourself (2)
here (I)
  look / listen —! (6)
  right — (12)
  up / down — (9)
herself (2)
Hey! (9)
to hide / hid / hidden (9)
to hijack /—ed /—ed
    (6)
hijacker(s) (6)

hijacking(s) (6)
hill(s) (12)
himself (2)
to hire /—d /—d (3)
history (10)
to hit / hit / hit (II)
hit(s) (2)
to hold / held / held (6)
home (I)
  back — (3)
  to leave — (17)
honestly (19)
Honor: Your — (10)
to hope /—d /—d (II)
horrible (11)
hour (I)
  half — (14)
  — after — (8)
How did (it) go? (19)
howdy (3)
to hug /—ged /—ged (I)
hung up see to hang
    up
to hurt / hurt / hurt (II)
hurt: to get — (6)

if I were you (13)
to import /—ed /—ed
    (12)
in (I)
  — + time (4)
  to be — (5)
  — fact (4)
  — my (your, etc.)
    opinion (20)
  — office (15)
  — order to (15)
  — the way (3)
  to move — (16)
including (4)
incredible (12)
indigestion (2)
industry (industries)
    (3)
inflation (13)
to inform /—ed /—ed
    (15)
information (15)
the inside (16)
insurance (4)
to intend /—ed /—ed
    (II)
to interrupt /—ed /—ed
    (20)

to interview /—ed /—ed (8)
interview(s) (7)
to invent /—ed /—ed (12)
invention(s) (12)
to invest /—ed /—ed (13)
investment(s) (15)
investor(s) (15)
to invite /—d /—d (II)
to iron /—ed /—ed (II)
itself (2)

jam (18)
jar(s) (18)
job(s) (I)
to lose a — (10)
joke(s) (2)
journey(s) (11)
judge(s) (1)
to jump /—ed /—ed (II)

to keep / kept / kept (II)
— in touch (1)
to — something + adj. (4)
kid(s) (1)
kidding: You're —! (1)
to kill /—ed /—ed (II)
kilometer(s) (4)
king(s) (14)
to kiss /—ed /—ed (I)
kiss(es) (9)
knew see to know
to knock (on) /—ed / —ed (16)
to know / knew / known (I)
to let someone — (5)

lace(s) (2)
lain see to lie
to land /—ed /—ed (II)
to last /—ed /—ed (II)
later: See you — (5)
latest (12)
to laugh /—ed /—ed (2)
to launch /—ed /—ed (10)

lawn(s) (14)
lawnmower(s) (14)
lawyer(s) (1)
lay see to lie
lazy (10)
to learn /—ed /—ed (II)
least (II)
at — (8)
leather (12)
to leave / left / left (I)
to — home (17)
to — someone alone (14)
to — something to someone (17)
left adv. (14); see also to leave
to lend / lent / lent (something to someone) (II)
to let / let / let (14)
— me see (5)
to — someone know (5)
liar(s) (19)
to lie / lay / lain (II)
to lie /—d /—d (19)
lie(s) (19)
to light / lit / lit (10)
light(s) (11)
to like /—d /—d (I)
like (I;II)
to feel — + -ing (7)
likewise (1)
to listen to /—ed /—ed (I)
— here! (6)
lit see to light
litter (3)
little (I)
for very — (20)
to live /—d /—d (I)
lock(s) (18)
to look /—ed /—ed (II)
to — forward to (3)
— here! (6)
— who's talking! (9)
loose (2)
to lose / lost / lost (II)
to — a job (10)
lousy (19)
to love /—d /—d (I)

luck (1)
Good —! (8)
to wish someone the best of — (1)
lumberyard(s) (20)

machine(s) (14)
mad (14)
made see to make
— from / of (12)
to mail /—ed /—ed (I)
to make / made / made (I)
to — friends (7)
to — matters worse (18)
to — someone + adj. (14)
to — someone do something (19)
to — up (your) mind(s) (7)
make-up (2)
to manage /—d /—d (7;16)
to manufacture /—d / —d (12)
marketing (5)
to marry / married / mar- ried (1)
matter(s) (5)
to make —s worse (18)
to mean / meant / meant (3)
I — (10)
means of transporta- tion (12)
meant see to mean
Mediterranean (Sea) (17)
medium(-sized) (4)
to meet / met / met (I)
to mess up /—ed up / —ed up (9)
mess(es) (10)
message(s) (5)
messy (9)
met see to meet
metal(s) (11)
to milk /—ed /—ed (14)
to mind /—ed /—ed (II)

to — your own business (20)
never — (9)
mind(s): to make up (your) —(s) (7)
to miss /—ed /—ed (II)
money (I)
to raise — (20)
more: What — . . .? (13)
to move /—d /—d (7)
to — in / out (16)
to mow /—ed /—ed (14)
myself (2)

nail(s) (20)
nearly (9)
neat (9)
necessary (15)
to need /—ed /—ed (I)
neither (II;3)
— . . . nor (6)
nervous (8)
never (II)
— mind (9)
new (I;II)
That's nothing —! (17)
news (I)
to break the — (15)
nice (I)
It was — talking to you (1)
—ly (7)
night watchman (men) (18)
noise(s) (4)
nonsense (17)
nor: neither . . . — (6)
not half as + adj. / adv. + as (7)
nothing (I)
for — (20)
That's — new! (17)
to notice /—d /—d (16)
now (I)
for — (12)
— and then (16)
a number of (16)

nylon (12)

occasion(s) (14)
off (II)
  — and on (10)
  — you go! (12)
to offer /—ed /—ed (15)
office(s) (I)
  in — (15)
officer(s) (14)
oil (4)
old (I;1)
on (I)
  to go — (10)
  off and — (10)
  — purpose (10)
  — sale (2)
  — the road (8)
  — the way (18)
  — time (5)
  to tell — (19)
to open /—ed /—ed (I)
  to — up (19)
opinion(s) (20)
  in my (your, etc.)
    — (20)
opportunity (oppor-
    tunities) (7)
or (I)
  either . . . — (5)
  — else (6)
order: in — to (15)
order(s) (5)
ordinary (12)
to organize /—d /—d
    (15)
orphanage(s) (20)
otherwise (15)
ought to (20)
ourselves (2)
out (II)
  to be — (5)
  to move — (16)
  — of the way (3)
  to put — a fire
    (10)
  to run — of (4)
  to wear — (9)
the outside (16)
oven(s) (2)
over (I;II)
  all — adv. (1); adj.
    (6)

to ask someone
    — (18)
to own /—ed /—ed (16)
own adj. (1)
  to mind your —
    business (20)
owner(s) (16)

paid see to pay
to paint /—ed /—ed (9)
to park /—ed /—ed (12)
passenger(s) (6)
to pay / paid / paid (II)
  to — attention (6)
pay (8)
to pedal /—ed /—ed
    (12)
per cent (15)
personally (20)
Peru (3)
photocopier(s) (18)
to pick up /—ed up /
    —ed up (II)
piece(s) (11)
to plan /—ned /—ned
    (II)
planet(s) (10)
to plant /—ed /—ed
    (15)
plastic (12)
to play /—ed /—ed (I)
pleased (II;5)
plenty (of) (4)
pliers (20)
plumber(s) (1)
plumbing (16)
plus (4)
point: to get to a / the
    — (where)
    (10)
pollution (7)
the poor (15)
poor (I;1)
position(s) (7;13)
  in a difficult — (13)
positive (17)
possibly (17)
to pray /—ed /—ed (6)
to predict /—ed /—ed
    (17)
prediction(s) (17)
to prefer /—red /—red
    (I)

previous (16)
prince(s) (14)
princess(es) (14)
probably (4)
to produce /—d /—d
    (12)
programmer(s): com-
    puter — (1)
to promise /—d /—d
    (II)
to protect (from) /—ed /
    —ed (12)
to pull /—ed /—ed (6)
purpose: on — (10)
to push /—ed /—ed (6)
to put / put / put (II)
  to — away (9)
  to — out a fire
    (10)

queen(s) (14)
quite (II;16)

radiator(s) (4)
to rain /—ed /—ed (I)
rainstorm(s) (10)
to raise /—d /—d (12)
  to — money (20)
rang see to ring
rat(s) (11)
rather (than) (13)
  would — (13)
razor blade(s) (2)
to read / read / read (I)
real (16)
real estate (I;II;13)
to realize /—d /—d (16)
reason(s) (10)
recipe(s) (2)
to redecorate /—d /—d
    (16)
to reduce /—d /—d (6)
to reelect /—ed /—ed
    (15)
to refuse /—d /—d (II)
relative(s) (17)
to remember /—ed /
    —ed (II)
to rent /—ed /—ed (I)
repairman (men) (1)
to report /—ed /—ed
    (I)

report(s) (5)
research (12)
responsibility (respon-
    sibilities) (20)
to rest /—ed /—ed (I)
result(s) (15)
to return /—ed /—ed
    (4)
reward(s) (15)
to ride / rode / ridden
    (II)
right (II)
  to go — (18)
  — here / there
    (12)
to ring / rang / rung (II)
road(s) (II)
  on the — (8)
  up / down the —
    (16)
to roast /—ed /—ed (9)
to rob /—bed /—bed
    (II)
rode see to ride
roof(s) (16)
room (I;20)
to run / ran / run (I)
  to — away (6)
  to — out of (4)
rung see to ring

safe(s) (18)
said see to say
  easier — than
    done (20)
to sail /—ed /—ed (3)
sailing: to go — (3)
sailor(s) (1)
sake:
  for Heaven's —
    (20)
  for (someone)'s
    — (20)
sale(s) (2)
  for — (16)
  on — (2)
sand (3)
sang see to sing
sat see to sit
to save /—d /—d (8)
saw see to see
saw(s) (20)
to say / said / said (II)

Index

Numbers refer to lessons, not pages.